ODYSSEYS OF SURVIVAL

46 Prisoners, 40 Years, 4 Wars

Julia D. Brodie, Ph.D.
and
Sandra Peeler Ellinger

ABOUT THE AUTHORS

Julia D. Brodie, Ph.D., has more than 45 years of experience as a professional psychologist and psychotherapist. Her interest in stress and stress management grew as she helped client after client deal with stress-related issues. Her reputation in this field led to pro bono workshops in Georgia for Habitat for Humanity and in Pennsylvania for the Mennonite Central Committee (MCC). Those original sessions led to additional pro bono work in Africa for service-workers with Habitat and the MCC as well as Church World Service and Catholic World Relief. Two trips, in 1988 and 1990, took her to Zambia, Zimbabwe, Kenya and Zaire.

Sandra P. Ellinger is a freelance writer. She previously was ghostwriter for the Carl Upchurch book Convicted in the Womb: One Man's Journey from Prisoner to Peacemaker (Bantam Books, 1996). Over the course of an 18-year career at Denison University, she was a speechwriter for two university presidents, wrote nominations for award consideration and profiles of award winners, and had an article published in the Denison Magazine.

by Julia D. Brodie, Ph.D. and Sandra P. Ellinger
Published by PhoenixGraphix.us
Produced with the support of William W. Davison, Ph.D.
Printed in the United States of America
ISBN: 978-0-9889971-5-8

DEDICATION

To "Bill" Brodie,
the light of my life,
for his unwavering love,
support and encouragement.

Odysseys

TABLE OF CONTENTS

Odysseys

INTRODUCTION

Thoughts about the nature of memory from Holocaust survivor, Jacob Hennenberg, eloquently illustrate why I felt compelled to write this book.

"Survivors can do as they please. They can be silent, lecture, publish their stories. All of these contribute to the future 'memory.' But memory is more than information, it is more than words. Memory is also a type of belief, internalized knowledge that comes not from understanding, but from experience. Memories and the certain knowledge that goes with them, will be gone forever once there are no more survivors. I cannot transfer my memory to you. But I can give you a memory of my memory. One day, perhaps 30 years from now, when no survivors are left, it will be your turn to speak for us. You will say that you were present when a survivor was witness and made you a witness for the witness. And when you are no longer able to speak, then the next generation will speak for you. This way, a thousand years from now, someone will stand and be a witness to a living memory." (Jacob Hennenberg. Self-published memoir, date unknown).

When I sat down with Jacob, I was about halfway through my personal odyssey—four years of crisscrossing the country to conduct the interviews that are the heart of this book. It offers you two unique features, the breadth of my research cohort and the striking commonality of survivors' experiences across the decades. My conversations with forty-six survivors whose experiences span forty years and four wars yielded a treasure-trove of raw experiences and hard-won wisdom. The stories, often presented in their own words, range from gut-wrenching to heart-warming. Collectively, their impact jumps off the page.

At heart, I am an explorer for whom the possibilities inherent in the unknown are irresistible. Even after forty-five years as a successful psychologist/psychotherapist with a strong background in stress and stress management, I wasn't nearly ready to retire. Because I loved my work, I opted instead to go exploring, and decided to expand my professional horizons by taking an in-depth look at stress outside the boundaries of day-to-day therapy sessions. I quickly found myself outside the boundaries of civilized life, focusing on three seemingly disparate groups of non-criminal prisoners—Holocaust survivors, ex-prisoners of war, and former political prisoners.

Being arrested, no matter the circumstances, can be traumatic. But all arrests are not the same. For example, someone arrested in the United States for allegedly committing a crime has access to family and friends, can hire or be given an attorney, has the ability to be out on bail while awaiting a fair trial, an orderly justice system with the opportunity to appeal the verdict, and a well-regulated penal system. Such was not the case for any of our non-criminal prisoners. The ex-POWs were actively waging war—from Germany to Japan, Korea to Vietnam—when they were taken captive by enemy combatants in retaliation for their actions. Two of my three political prisoners deliberately put themselves in harm's way. With no thought for their own safety, each worked openly to depose what he considered to be an unethical and amoral government. The third political prisoner was simply the victim of circumstance: wrong place, wrong time. The Jews were neither armed soldiers at war nor political dissidents. They were simply citizens who did nothing to precipitate the calamities that befell them under Hitler, who transmuted their Jewish birthright into a sin against society, grievous enough to warrant the attempted extermination of the entire race. Over the course of my interviews, these three different routes to the status of non-criminal prisoner merged into the common task of somehow learning to survive the severe stresses of captivity.

So, why am I the perfect person to write this book? My own story begins with two encounters, fifty years apart. I met Marian Anderson in 1939, when I was ten years old. I saw Nelson Mandela in 1990, when I was 60. They are the heroes of my life, my role models and my inspiration. Anderson introduced me to the indignities of racial prejudice and Mandela exemplified the fight against it. I am a social justice activist and author because of them.

A ten-year-old Julia meets Marian Anderson (1939)

In 1945, while Anderson and Mandela were each enduring the racial prejudice of their own time and place, I was 16 years old, attending Mansfield (Ohio) High School. My burgeoning civil-rights interests spurred me and the only one of my friends with similar views on social activism, Virginia McMichael, to join the school's Inter-racial Youth Forum. I had a first-hand experience with Jim Crow laws when I and my mixed-race group of friends tried to go out and eat. For whatever reason, we were all full of ourselves that day and decided to go to the Mansfield Leland Hotel, the classiest place in town. In the hotel coffee shop, we all looked at the menu and told the man behind the counter what we wanted. He took a long look at us and said sure, he could pour a Coca Cola for Herbie, my African-American friend, then casually added, "I'll have to break the glass afterwards." Years later, when I read Marian Anderson's autobiography, I felt a strong empathy for a teenaged girl hoping to get into a prestigious music school, but hearing instead, "We don't take colored."

In the fall of 1947, I got on the train and headed off to college at Northwestern University, confident of my intelligence and clueless about almost everything else. I did well in my courses, and fell in love with the man who became my first husband. I saw him every weekend, and halfway through my senior year, we were married. Based on my years of education and counseling (and not a little bit of hindsight), I can now diagnose as "generalized anxiety" the strange rash that broke out on my face and arms each time a weekend visit with my boyfriend approached, and just as mysteriously disappeared when I went back to campus on Sunday evenings. The therapist I consulted to help me work through the stress informed me I simply needed to learn "mature female dependence"—thinly disguised academic language for "Know your place, my dear." I transferred to Syracuse University to be with my new husband and finish my degree, and I'm proud to say that I was a good wife and a good mother in spite of never having had any interest in mastering "mature female dependence."

In 1961, I had a series of sessions with another psychotherapist to explore some childhood issues, during which I learned that my mother, for all her gifts, had been emotionally unavailable to me. As I began to search for ways to compensate for that lack, I came to understand, at age 32, that I had control of my own life. I could decide what I wanted to do and be, personally and professionally. I took myself back to school to become a psychologist/psychotherapist and eventually found great personal satisfaction in being a therapist—a profession all about feelings, about being present and supportive, about nurturing personal strength and emotional resilience in my clients.

During my career, I found myself particularly interested in how you and I experience and manage loss, stress and traumatic stress—a concentration that stemmed partly from the loss of a hoped-for career as a concert pianist, partly from the stresses of my first marriage, and partly from watching my mother struggle with stress. She died in 1957, after battling chronic stress-related stomach ulcers, never having had access to the stress-management techniques I used and taught throughout my career. And while I treasure the memory of all those I was able to help, I deeply regret that my expertise in the field came too late to do the same for my own mother.

After an interesting and informative stretch as a staff psychologist at a mental-health clinic, I ended up with a successful private practice specializing in stress and stress management. Along the way, I got divorced (at age 45), learned to sail (at age 47), remarried (at age 49), learned to alpine ski and snorkel and scuba dive (at age 65). I got it into my head to do stress-management workshops in Africa, home of my hero, Nelson Mandela. My second husband and I took two trips there, doing workshops for Habitat for Humanity, the Mennonite Central Committee, Church World Service and Catholic World Relief in Zambia, Zimbabwe, Kenya and Zaire. While I was there, I had the joy of seeing Mandela up close, in a motorcade shortly after his release from prison.

Professionally, I continued to explore the common denominators in loss and feeling powerless, something I had dealt with not only in my own life but in many client sessions, especially with parents who had lost children, those who were subjected to spousal abuse, and abused children. When a friend told me she knew a former political prisoner from Taiwan, it occurred to me there could well be similarities between non-criminal prisoners and my clients, both of whom were coping with circumstances over which they had had no control. When I was offered the opportunity to interview the Taiwanese man, I eagerly accepted. Two years later, I met and interviewed a Holocaust survivor. Another two years passed before a third interview occurred, this time with an ex-prisoner of war. Notes, audio tapes and the recorded transcripts from those three conversations were each tucked away, with no particular project in mind.

Everything changed in August 2000, during my annual two-week stay at the Chautauqua Institute in western New York State. I had an unexpected and life-changing meeting with Ahmed Kathrada, a member of Nelson Mandela's inner circle of compatriots. After Kathrada's lecture, the explorer in me, along with my natural assertiveness, prompted me to go to the front of the lecture hall and introduce myself. I told him I was a psychologist very interested in stress and would greatly appreciate a chance to speak with him further about his experiences during the long years he and Mandela had been imprisoned at Robben Island in South Africa. Kathrada agreed to meet with me later that day.

Our conversation brought back vivid memories of my excitement at seeing Mandela, ten years before. Kathrada's many years as Mandela's right-hand man had made him adept at being an accomplished surrogate when the occasion required it. He kept bringing Mandela into our interview, evoking his presence in the room and saying his name in that unique South African musical cadence, running the syllables together so "Mr. Mandela" always sounded like "mistermandela." Hearing first-hand from Kathrada about his and Mandela's experiences generated a high level of interest and excitement in me. In a watershed moment, I realized that my training and my passions about social justice had come together.

As my husband and I drove home from Chautauqua that summer of 2000, questions were racing through my mind. In processing the history, present experiences and future expectations of successive life situations, which psychological factors interact most effectively to contribute to survival? What types of events are catalysts for physiological and psychological stress reactions? What can change unsuccessful coping into productive action? How do people endure years of imprisonment? As I mulled over these questions, I made a decision to act on the strong impulse I had felt after speaking with Kathrada, and committed myself then and there to an exploration of the ways in which non-criminal prisoners manage to sustain themselves in the face of loss and stress.

The next eight months were spent building a list of interview prospects and fine-tuning the questions I wanted to ask. On May 8, 2001, I conducted my first official interview. Since I was still working, it took me almost four years to the day before I finished the last of forty-six interviews. My heartfelt gratitude goes out to those brave men and women who were willing to share their memories. Sadly for them, the old intellectual memories were often accompanied by painful feelings, sometimes with great intensity. Their willingness to revisit experiences no one should have to go through even once makes the gift of candid interviews by these former prisoners even more precious.

To fully inhabit Jacob Hennenberg's vision of "a witness for the witness," you need to have a rudimentary understanding of the nuances of stress and change, and how they function within the culture of prisons (Chapter One). Armed with that knowledge, you will readily grasp how important the two principle stress-management strategies—inter- and intrapersonal support—were to everyone's survival (Chapters Two and Three). I then give you several lenses through which to view the survivors' stories, including the influence of religion, how it felt to be the recipient of unimagined gestures of kindness, the surprising ways in which desperation fuels creativity, and the hard years, even decades, that following being liberated from their prisons (Chapter Four through Seven). The final chapter will briefly offer thoughts about what I learned from these survivors and how they have changed my life.

Excerpts from the survivors' interviews are woven through the narrative of each chapter. As you come across their quoted words, you will notice some departures from accepted English grammar and sentence construction. Their inclusion is intentional. During the interviews, I was as captivated by the "feel" of the conversations as I was by the stories themselves. These were informal occasions. I was welcomed into comfortable kitchens where I met friendly, supportive spouses. I was introduced to children and grandchildren via clusters of family photographs, and even met all the family pets. Reluctant to end the sharing of stories, we often went far beyond my list of questions. Listening to the foreign and U.S. regional accents, watching the survivors search for just the right words, stopping myself from helping them when the thought being expressed was especially difficult to say—all served to make each interview unique. For all those reasons, I have chosen to reproduce their English just as they said it, the better to capture the essence of their experiences and their personalities.

Odysseys

1

CONTEXT: STRESS, CHANGE AND
THE CULTURE OF PRISONS

Between 1933 and 1945, the Nazi regime built approximately twenty thousand detention facilities to imprison and eliminate so-called "enemies of the state." The camps were used for a range of purposes that included forced-labor camps, transit camps that served as temporary way stations, and extermination camps built primarily or exclusively for mass murder. Most prisoners in the early concentration camps were German Communists, Socialists, Social Democrats, Gypsies, Jehovah's Witnesses, homosexuals and persons accused of "asocial" or socially deviant behavior. These facilities were called "concentration camps" because those imprisoned there were physically "concentrated" in one location. Henry Greenbaum's story, which follows, puts a face—a child's face, at that—on this brief description of Nazi camps.[1]

Henry and his family were taken into the ghetto when Henry was only 11 years old. He progressed through a series of labor camps during the next five years before the family, along with everyone else from the ghetto, was packed into open railroad cars. They all believed the rumor that they were being moved to protect them from the Russians coming in from the East as well as from the Allied bombing raids. When the doors of the cattle cars opened, reality began to dawn. Henry's description of their arrival at what they later learned was Auschwitz is chilling: "They packed us in the railroad cars and on the way we had dead people in the aisles and people were all tangled. When we arrived at Auschwitz, we had to push to get out. They were screaming, 'Aus! Aus!' 'Get out! Get out!' There were dogs barking. And they were standing there, all well-dressed men, clean-shaven and, I hate to say, good-looking. The murderer was on the inside. It didn't show on the outside. They were standing there, smiling, but with little whips."

Henry was assigned to a barracks with other children. They all worked long hours and never had enough food to satisfy their nutritional needs, much less their teenaged appetites. Henry remembers that every time there was an air raid, when the non-Jews and the German guards would run for their bunker, his 16-year-old bunkmate would run for the kitchen, hoping to find some sour soup. One day, the guards came and picked out Henry's bunkmate and three others. Henry did not know what any of them had done, but he can never forget what was done to them. He told me, "We all came out of the larder to watch. They had one of the prisoners pull the levers on the back of the platform to make the floor drop away, and down they went, just hanging from the nooses. When they stopped shaking, the Germans started playing music. That's what got me. I said to myself, 'Over food, over food. It was just over food.' That's what did it. If he hadn't been going there, he'd survive."

When a German industrialist was permitted to select some healthy-looking prisoners for free labor at the I.G. Farber chemical factory, Henry was part of this group. The factory had been retooled to produce ammunition and Henry's job was taking newly made shells out of the oven. The shells were 36 inches long, shaped almost like a bottle, and it took two people to pick them up and set them carefully on end in a bed of sand so they could cool. One day, his friend put his end of the shell down crooked and the whole row went down. When the two boys got back to the camp, they were called out and taken into the guardhouse. Henry said, "They made us undress from the waist up and they put us in a chair. Our knees were on the floor, our chest was on the seat and our heads went right through the back. They beat us with a long whip and the more you cried, the more they beat you. Eventually, you didn't feel it any more. My back when I came out was like a roadmap of whip marks. It didn't take much time to break the skin; we were malnourished. They wouldn't let us put on our shirt. They held us up to the whole factory. Once we come out, everybody sees how beat up we got, but we didn't do that on purpose. It was an accident." When I asked Henry what he might have thought about to help him get through the beating, he said, "It was just a beating. At first you cry, then you grab the leg of the chair and just...shut up. They never stopped. I remember thinking, 'I hope I survive. I hope I survive.'"

The Weight of Stress

Most of our everyday living is a composite of normal ups and downs, minor stress points that we process almost automatically. Coping with higher stress levels require a higher degree of awareness. Over the years, I helped my clients learn to examine each stress event through three filters: past events, current feelings, and future hopes. The overall coping process, however, is not nearly as linear as the three filters would suggest. As well, broad definitions or broad examinations of stress may create a momentary illusion of stress management, but the most effective results come from doing the hard work of untangling a messy knot of interrelated stresses that likely took years to construct.

Even though the survivors didn't have the benefit of professional help, a thread runs through all their stories about change and loss and the weight of stress. Each one illustrates the interplay of three particular factors related to experiencing stress that affect not only the survivors but you and me as well: the influence of individual personality traits, the degree of threat perceived in any given situation, and the fact that stress is cumulative. The influence of individual personality traits is readily apparent in the multiple ways these survivors dealt with their circumstances. Those who were generally easy-going and adept at dealing with unexpected events, those who had the ability to roll with the punches, were much more likely to endure their hardships while maintaining manageable stress levels. Those who were accustomed to leading before being imprisoned assumed those same leadership roles in their new, more restrictive environments. The problem-solvers solved problems. The natural caregivers never lacked for opportunities to lessen someone else's burden. Among the children caught up in the crucible of war, personality development that might ordinarily occupy a decade or more could be compressed into half that time or less. As one of the Holocaust children said, "I was twelve when it was over, but I was maybe in my twenties in terms of coping skills."

The second common thread, the perceived degree of threat in any given situation, also has an enormous influence on stress levels. The survivors' day-to-day baseline stress levels were higher than most of us experience even in crisis mode. Whether they were simply trying to have a one-on-one conversation or work-ing with a large group to plan an escape attempt, they repeatedly weighed the potential consequences of being caught against the potential benefits of succeeding. The persistence of such defiant behavior in the face of terrible odds against them is remarkable. That persistence becomes almost heroic when we add in the third common factor, the cumulative nature of stress. Imagine taking the same risk every day—outwitting your guards to retrieve a hidden sandwich, talking to someone on the other side of a block wall, singing a quiet song at night, stealing food whenever you could—for two days in a row, or 20, or 200, or 2,000. The weight of the stress grows with each episode, adding to the depth of the desperation.

My own wartime experiences pale in comparison to what our survivors endured. I was in junior high and high school dur-ing World War II, safe and sound in Central Ohio, but I vividly remember the tension of December 7, 1941. I was twelve years old when I sat with my whole family, crowding around our big Philco radio to listen to the newscasters describe what was hap-pening halfway around the world. We all learned to deal with the rationing of sugar, coffee and gasoline, and my mother carefully saved all the bacon drippings and discarded fats from our daily cooking so they could be used in the production of gun powder.[2] When the major automakers stopped producing cars during the war and retooled their factories to make tanks, my dad's success-ful car dealership had nothing to sell—and people had nothing to buy—but used cars.

The Science of Stress

Knowledge of the broad effects of stress emerged in 1965 through the ground-breaking work of physiologist Hans Selye, the first scientist to identify the "fight-or-flight" reaction, a term that refers to the heightened levels of tension and alertness that occur when a stressful event is experienced. Selye's work was a huge step in understanding the ways humans and other mammals react to stress, and it was the first to reveal changes in the adrenal glands of laboratory rats after the animals had been subjected to laboratory-induced stress.[3] In a deceptively simple experiment,

Selye subjected one group of rats to unpredictable experiences related to feeding, while a control group experienced a normal, more predictable feeding experience. Selye later determined that the adrenal glands of the rats that experienced more feeding frustrations (i.e., more stress) were much larger than the adrenal glands in the control group. Thus it was seen that even small animals will experience physiological changes in their bodies because of difficult life experiences (Selye, 1976).

Studies with human subjects followed, confirming and expanding on Selye's findings. This important information soon caught the interest of the general public. The 1960s and '70s saw the beginning of stress-management workshops as well as books and articles on the topic. While Selye's work was emerging, I was in the early stages of my career and found myself increasingly drawn to the study and treatment of stress, often defined as the natural or gradual "wear and tear" on the mind and body. We know that the effects of stress are not always noticeable at first but over time they can have a significant impact, both psychologically and physically. Research continues to produce additional information of what precipitates stress, how it affects us, and how best to manage it.

Besides Selye's work, there were two other strong influences on my career. The first was cognitive therapy,[4] along with the concept of self-talk. The second was Gestalt Theory, which had been in use for about a decade by the mid-1960s as a lens through which to study human stress and its corollary, stress management. Gestalt Theory and the Gestalt Cycle of Experience were particularly suited to my work with loss and stress. I studied Perls and his description of Gestalt Theory. He said, "Gestalt therapy is not so interested in questions of where development may have been arrested in a patient's childhood as in helping identify and work through the present anxieties and blocks…that prevent… growth from taking place" (Perls, 1994). Ever assertive, I did not totally agree with Perls' definition of Gestalt Theory, convinced by my experiences with clients that the interplay of personal history with Gestalt Theory enriched their experience and led to productive outcomes.

In therapy sessions, I often observed the stages of the Gestalt Cycle of Experience as they played out over the course of numerous therapy sessions. The Cycle, commonly represented as a circle, is an eight-stage process: sensation, awareness, energy, mobilization, action, contact, closure, withdrawal (Nevis, 1987). It can apply to an experience that continues over several years, e.g., the total time of being a prisoner, or an event that lasts only moments. Our everyday lives are filled with such cycles of experience, whether we notice them or not. Fortunately for us, Nevis and others did notice those cycles and formalized the progression of steps; the result is now a widely accepted component of Gestalt Theory.

Let me illustrate the Cycle using my experience of seeing Nelson Mandela.

- *Sensation*: I was physically excited at the chance to actually see Mandela in person.
- *Awareness*: I was thrilled to be in that huge crowd and also was very aware that I was the only white person there.
- *Energy*: I was energized by the roar of the crowd, first in the distance, then growing ever closer and louder as the motorcade neared where I was standing.
- *Mobilization*: I am a small woman and badly wanted to get to where I could see the motorcade.
- *Action*: I made my way through the crowd, up to the front, with the help of bystanders, who were pleased to see a white person there with them.
- *Contact*: As Mandela's motorcade drove by, I jumped into the air (wearing a bright yellow blouse) and yelled; our eyes met and he smiled at me.
- *Closure*: He was gone in a few seconds, but I had done what I wanted and needed to do.
- *Withdrawal*: Still on an emotional high from the experience, I made my way back to the guest house where I was staying.

Closure was in short supply for our survivors, and withdrawal was not an option selected by any of them. Rather, they endured a series of truncated Cycles of Experience that only served to increase their stress levels. This common experience led to the conclusions that form the basis of this book: stress is impervious to geography, to politics or to one's station in life, and successful stress-management techniques transcend the specifics of place and person. Similar behaviors quickly became apparent through the course of my conversations with survivor after survivor. Regardless of their specific setting, they were all non-criminal prisoners facing common stresses and surviving common dangers. They learned the same lessons about how to survive and they were all strong enough, and lucky enough, to be alive on their respective liberation days.

To truly understand their stressors, however, we need to get specific. Consider generalized anxiety, for example. With no clear-cut information, it is easy to imagine the worst, and the survivors saw enough horrifying things to make "the worst" their most obvious conclusion. Compared to their former lives, the predictable became unpredictable. Normal became abnormal, certainty became uncertainty, order became chaos. Prisoners were subjected to unremitting stress, day in and day out. Regardless of the specific stressors of any given moment, anxiety pervaded every corner of their lives. That's what generalized anxiety is, an unfocused pall that hangs over everything. It is not about a particular event or experience or trigger. You just feel anxious but don't know exactly why (DSM-IV, 1994; see References, page 166).

Then there are the "Which cliff?" decisions. When you have nothing left to lose, you make different decisions than you might make when you still have some hope. With your back to the wall and faced with equally undesirable options, you are forced to make a "which cliff" choice. While such decisions made in my client sessions were rarely, if ever, about life-and-death circumstances, I can report with certainty that they felt that way to the clients who wrestled with those choices. For our survivors, on the other hand, it was all about deciding how to die. Did they passively stay where they were and wait for the end, or did they take a wild risk, knowing they might be killed in the process? My Taiwanese political activist, knowing that he would spend the rest of his life under house arrest, captured the essence of the dilemma when he said, "I feared my life was in danger. Since that kind of life was not worth living, it was worth taking the risk to escape."

My youngest former political prisoner was not a political activist at all, but his experience exemplifies generalized anxiety. *James* was a doctoral student from Yale University, working on his doctoral degree. He was in the midst of his final trip to Germany, putting the finishing touches on his dissertation during the Cold War in the early 1960s. From 1959-61 he lived and worked in West Berlin. Since work on the Berlin Wall did not begin until August of 1961, *James* was able to complete approximately three dozen interviews in East Berlin and also visit a number of East Berlin libraries to read pertinent materials unavailable in the West. Near the end of August 1961, the dissertation was complete. On August 25, *James* went over to East Berlin one last time to thank an East German economist who had been helping him start on a new project and to let her know that the worsening political situation had convinced him to cancel their joint research.

He had no idea that the woman had fled to the West a few days before and, as a result, the East German secret police, the Stasi, had staked out her apartment. They arrested *James* on suspicion of assisting in her escape and seized his car and its contents, including his dissertation. After a few days of "interviews" and after translating his dissertation into German, the Stasi had a good idea of *James's* activities over the last two years and the original charge soon became a charge of espionage, based loosely on the economic-trade nature of his dissertation. The charge did not hold up and almost six months later, on February 19, 1962, the East German attorney general issued an order for *James* to be released. The actual release did not occur for another month when *James* and Francis Gary Powers, the U.S. pilot taken captive when he flew his fighter over East German territory, were traded for convicted Soviet spy, Colonel Abel.

Thirty years later, in 1992, *James* applied to see his Stasi file, which he received a year-and-a-half later. It contained his dissertation (beautifully translated into German), reports from five months of daily interrogations; reports about every piece of paper in his car, his wallet and his pockets; and a full transcript of a pre-release conversation with his attorney that he had always considered to be private. Even after all those years, reading his file took *James* back to the anxiety he had felt during those six months of imprisonment. In that reading room, he kept having to remind himself that thirty-one years had passed since those events took place. He told me, "I began to experience many of the fears that I had during my interrogations: a general anxiety, a fear that I might have hurt other people, and a hopelessness. I felt again what it was like in my cell, and the efforts I took to maintain some type of mental equilibrium." To gain control and perspective over the distressing memories, *James* instinctively retreated to the same emotional safe zone he had used at the time—an elementary-school classroom where he tried to remember everyone in his third-grade class.

Holocaust survivors were political pawns. Joe Diamond's story clearly illustrates that he and his fellow prisoners were regarded with no more consideration of their humanity than if they had been game pieces on a chessboard. Joe was born in the east part of Czechoslovakia in 1929. The first ten years of his life in Seredne, a small town of nearly 20,000 people, were pretty ordinary, probably very similar to the way we feel about our own lives today. He lived with his mother, father and little brother, Arie. His family owned a farm, a grocery store and a clothing store. In 1939, when World War II began, Czechoslovakia was still an ally of the United States and England. But once Hungary occupied the country, the Czech government became a German Nazi puppet government. Laws against the Jews began, as did pograms, which were organized massacres of Jews. All Jews, including children, were required to wear a yellow Star of David at all times to differentiate them from the rest of the Caucasian population.

It was 1944 before the Seredne town crier announced that everyone with any Jewish heritage must pack minimal belongings and be prepared to be taken away within the next 24 hours. All Jewish people were declared a security risk and were told they would be taken to a German farm to work on the harvest. The next morning, Joe and his family were ready. Two storm

troopers came into his house with fixed bayonets to take them
to a local school for processing. The 600 people there, including
Joe's family, were no longer simply citizens of Seredne. They were
now prisoners. The soldiers searched them for valuables and Joe
remembers an officer sticking his hand inside a baby's mouth to
check for any hidden gold. Thirty German soldiers surrounded
the group as they walked down the streets. The whole non-Jewish
population of the town was watching, like it was a parade, with
no concern or anxiety. Joe vividly recalls a man chewing tobacco,
spitting on the ground and saying, "It's about time to get rid of
those Jewish people."

Everyone was taken by train to a ghetto in a remote aban-
doned factory building where they lived in tents with no running
water. Joe's description of the ghetto illustrates that ambiguous
situations, full of generalized unease or even fear, are unnerving:
"When the Jews were concentrated into ghettos, they had no way
to find out exactly what was happening. All information from
the outside—radios, newspapers, telephones—was banned. The
ghetto newspaper never addressed what was happening in the
world. The social "grapevine," usually a reliable source of information about virtually anything and everything, was cut off."

After four weeks, the group was taken to the railway station
and packed into cattle cars with barely room enough to stand.
The train headed east, toward Poland, instead of west to Germany
and those rumored farms. When the train finally stopped and
the doors were opened, everyone was faced with three German
officers who said, "Good morning. Welcome to Auschwitz," or
"Work will make you free." This was the first time they had ever
heard the name "Auschwitz." Everyone was told to stand in one of
two lines to be interviewed to see what kind of work they could
do, and Joe remembers thinking that made sense. The men were
in one line, women and children under age seven in the other.
With no chance to even say goodbye, Joe and his father were sent
to the labor camp. They were told they could visit his mother
and brother on weekends but they later learned that within three
hours of arriving at Auschwitz, the two had been sent to the gas
chambers and killed. After a week, Joe's father was sent to Buch-

enwald where he did slave labor on railroads, carrying rocks and wheeling coal. Joe didn't see his father again until after liberation.

Joe described a pervasive experience among his fellow prisoners, that of being made to feel non-human: "Everyone wore the same 'uniform.' Everyone's head was shaved. Everyone was weak from hunger all the time. And everyone got an ID number tattooed onto their arm, along with instructions to forget their given names."

Change and Stress

Change is so deeply intertwined with stress that each can be a component of the other. Even so, there are some key differences between the two. Change almost inevitably leads to stress, while stress is an emotional and physiological reaction to change. Some people thrive on and even choose a certain level of stress. I am one of those people, at least in the areas of exploring new ideas. Opting to return to college at the age of thirty-two and eventually earn advanced degrees in counseling and clinical psychology brought me exciting new challenges, as well as some stress. I can personally attest that even though many planned changes are welcome, they still can generate a certain measure of stress.

I have dealt with both unwelcome and unplanned change in my life, but I have never been arrested. Even so, I know that, regardless of the circumstances, every instance of arrest initiates unwelcome change imposed by the momentum of events out of your control. This can result in exponential increases in stress levels, forcing you into unfamiliar territory and altering your usual decision-making routines. When the nth degree of "unfamiliar territory" becomes the norm of daily life, the resulting stress could push prisoners into giving up. Those who did so engaged in behaviors that ranged from throwing themselves against electrified fences to retreating inwards to the point of unresponsiveness. Those prisoners who somehow kept desperation at bay are represented by the men and women of my interview list. The stories that follow come from both POWs and civilian non-combatants, each swept up by traumatic and sudden waves of change.

The change was perhaps most abrupt for four military men engaged in the air war: Dick Mann, *Harry*, *Hank* and Claude

Watkins. Each functioned as a member of a close-knit and well-trained crew. Three of the four had to bail out when their planes were hit and each of them was thrust out into the cold, jolting slipstream. The fourth managed to land his plane safely and lead his crew away from the area. All their stories give us a glimpse into the uncertainty of that slice of time between fighting man and prisoner of war, when neither life nor death is certain. Each man literally had only minutes to make a rapid and difficult transition from the role of highly competent decision-maker to that of prisoner.

Dick Mann, who was a Navy pilot in the Pacific during World War II, ended up in Ofuna prison camp. Ofuna, never listed as an official POW prison, was an interrogation center primarily for aircrews. Prisoners slept on filthy straw mats on the floor. Conditions were inhuman, as verified by a Red Cross official who visited the camp on August 24, 1945, two days before release and said it was the worst he had ever seen. Medical attention was nonexistent. The only food was a small bowl of rice or barley three times a day.[5]

On the day he was captured, Dick's squadron had been flying a mission to strike shipping in the Kure area. They pushed over into their dives at approximately 13,000 feet, headed straight down for a Japanese heavy cruiser in the harbor below. Dick dove almost vertically to 1,500 feet, then released his bombs—a 1,000-pound G.P. and a 260-pound frag bomb. Both scored direct hits. On the pull-out, a Japanese gunner scored a direct hit of his own. The left wing of Dick's plane burned so badly he was forced to ditch in Kure Harbor. He and his radioman-gunner, Hanna, got out of the plane with relatively minor injuries and were picked out of the water by a Japanese fishing boat.

The beatings began before they even reached the shore. Both were tied up, laid on the boat's deck on their backs, and kicked in the face. Once on land, two guards were placed over each man, and a forced march began. Dick described it for me: "We were marched for two miles, through three villages, during which time the civilians had a free-for-all. It seemed that every person in the mob who had lost a friend or relative in the war was using this opportunity to get revenge. Clubs, backs of swords, stones and most anything handy were used on us, so that by the time we reached a small house where they let us sit down, we were a mass of blood from head to foot. I can remember being knocked on my knees at least three times."

The two men were blindfolded and put aboard another fishing boat that took them to a jail. The next morning, the interrogation started in earnest. Dick remembers, "The information they wanted from me was very confidential so, upon my refusal to disclose it, I received severe beatings with a pole that looked and was swung much like an extra-long baseball bat. This went on all day." Finally, Dick was blindfolded again, put in a truck and taken to a different prison camp, where he was fed and spent the night. Next morning, he was fed again, loaded on the back of a truck and sent back to the interrogators. The questioning went on as before. Many of his answers were simply "I do not know." When they asked how many planes were on the strike the morning Dick was shot down, he said "75," knowing full well there must have been at least 150.

At that point, he was dragged from his chair, taken outside and forced far back into a cave dug into the side of a hill. His memory of what happened in the cave was still vivid: "They made me sit in the mud with my head up against a post while a murderous-looking Jap stood in readiness with a long, two-handled sword. My life had been threatened several times before, but when the interrogator said, 'Leftenant Mann, you have evaded our questions long enough. Now you are about to lose your head,' I realized I was in a serious predicament. I was again asked the same question. Since my answer was still '75,' I fully expected to see the executioner swing his weapon. Hanna was brought in at that time and asked the same question. While the Jap was squaring away to sever my head from my body, Hanna gave his answer of '75-80.' The interrogator informed the Jap with the sword to place it back in its scabbard, and I was marched out of the cave. Some days later, I learned from Hanna that, due to the echo effect of the cave, he had overheard my answer as he entered."

Harry's knowledge of the Norton bombsight led to him being assigned to the nose of a B-24 long-range bomber, flying missions from Southern Italy into the Balkans. As the lead bombardier, his job was to find the target and get it in the crosshairs. His plane was shot down on his 37th mission, over Vienna, on a day when there were high losses to his squadron from German 88mm cannon on the ground. *Harry* told me that when the crew bailed out, "The slipstream took the helmet right off my head. As we got lower and lower, I saw bicycles, hedges and houses. It was as if I was beside myself, looking at myself. I came on down and felt a big shock. I must have been knocked unconscious on the landing because when I woke up, I was surrounded by soldiers, and I knew from the movies they were Germans. One of them said to me, 'For you, the war is over.'"

Being taken prisoner was a shocking change. *Harry* had been totally focused on the success of his mission and, in the bat of an eye, was in a completely different environment: "Not one of us was prepared for the experience. You know absolutely nothing about what to expect. I had to learn to be a prisoner of war." Part of that learning took place on the trek from where *Harry* was captured to the POW camp where he would be held. Whether they were walking or herded into boxcars, "we were treated like animals, with no food, no water and just enough room to stand or maybe sit." After several days, *Harry* finally arrived at Stalag Luft III at Moosburg. He ended up in the North Compound, where the "Great Escape" originated (see Chapter Six for more details) and said he clearly remembered "the day they brought back ashes of the escapees who didn't make it out." The men were starving from the first day of camp, something none of them had experienced before. But that was only part of the stress. *Harry* added, "You never knew what to expect next. You could always hear the war, day and night, sometimes for several days, and we could see lights on aircraft above us at night. We worried, if the Allies broke through, whether they'd recognize us as friends or enemies."

Hank was also held in Stalag Luft III. The story of how he got there comes from a diary he kept at the time, which described the events the led up to his capture by the Nazis. *Hank* was a navigator aboard a U.S. bomber, flying his fifth mission over Berlin the day he was shot down. As he picked out his target, he felt a terrific hit just off the right side of the ship, up near the nose. When the pilot pulled out of the formation and started to dive, *Hank* instantly knew something was wrong. He told me, "The suddenness of the dive kept me glued to my seat and I knew we had had it! I figured that if I was going down, I at least should drop my bombs on the city, and I did." After "salvoing" the bombs, *Hank* turned around and saw the navigator at the hatch, his feet dangling, all set to bail out. *Hank* tumbled out of his seat, grabbed his chest-pack chute and hooked it on as he went up to the pilot's compartment to see if his friend, Hal, was okay. Hal calmly showed *Hank* the useless instruments, and both men knew they had no chance to bring the ship back home.

The two men headed for the escape hatch. When *Hank* sat down on the edge of the hatch, he suddenly noticed that his leg straps were unbuckled. He told me, "I started to buckle them when I felt a tap on my back, which clearly meant, 'Let's get the hell out of here!' because the ship was going fast." So *Hank* jumped without his chute properly rigged. The slipstream at 8,000 feet whipped him out into space and he immediately jerked the ripcord. His next words startled me: "Imagine my dismay when I saw the chute didn't open and all I had to look at was a handle in my hand, which I immediately flung away!" Just about then, *Hank* heard a terrific explosion and parts of the ship came tumbling past him. He continued, "I was just about to check in my cards and call it quits, when I realized how much I had to live for. Frantically, I clawed at my chute, ripped open the flap and started pulling out the silk. Suddenly, the chute blossomed with a terrific jerk and damn near threw me out of the harness. Since my leg straps weren't buckled, I was hanging on by means of my elbows and must have been at about 3,000 feet when the chute opened."

As he floated downwards, *Hank* could see countryside below him that looked peaceful. He was headed for a large wooded area and, before he knew it, founded himself hanging from a high tree that had snagged his chute. He dropped out of his harness—pretty simple to do since his leg straps had never been fastened—and landed with a thud. He couldn't get his chute out of the tree so, even though it was a marker for the Germans that someone had landed there, he left it and started running with no purpose but to get out of the area. He was eventually captured by the Nazis and held in a POW camp for about a year before liberation. His biggest worry during that year was that someone in charge would find out he was Jewish and ship him off to one of the concentration camps. Luckily, that fear never became a reality. *Hank* returned to Rochester, N.Y. after the war where he married, had a family, and became a college English professor.

Claude Watkins enlisted in 1942 and, once on active duty with the U.S. Army Air Forces,[6] flew B-17 missions over Europe in 1943-44 from his base in Suffolk, England. On February 10, 1944, the crew flew what was to be their 15 and last mission. Their target was an industrial area in Germany and they were one of a squadron of 169 bombers on the mission. Their expected air escort of 366 fighters (P-38s, 47s, and 51s) that would protect the bombers from the Luftwaffe over enemy territory never left England, grounded by bad weather. On the enemy side, the Luftwaffe 410s had clear skies, and Claude's aircraft was the last of five from his group to go down.

The men of Claude's crew left the aircraft at about 28,000 feet and pulled their rip cords at what Claude judged to be 15,000 feet. They drifted eastward while descending, and Claude remembers the sudden silence during the free fall and then under the chute as perhaps the most striking thing about the event. At about 500 feet off the ground, he drifted over a small village on a hill and could see people looking up at him. A little bit lower, the wind that was causing him to drift was cut off by a hill and he made a fairly straight drop into brush-covered broken rock. He and a friend were captured almost immediately—by a woman with a pitchfork and two young teenage boys with a rifle and a dog.

Claude couldn't put any weight on his left leg, so the two boys each took one of his arms over their shoulders and helped him up the hill to a barn. A few minutes later, some more villagers led a second member of Claude's crew, the lower-ball-turret gunner, into the barn. Luckily, he was able to give Claude a morphine injection with supplies from his escape-and-evasion kit. Shortly afterwards, two German soldiers, one Army and the other Air Force, arrived in a staff car. They took the two Americans to a fighter field near what would have been their target and, during the ride, had a good laugh over all the French francs the Americans had in their pocket escape-and-evasion kits. By the next day, all ten of Claude's crewmates had been rounded up and were in separate cells in the air base guard house.

Claude describes his experiences from this point on as "routine" for Eighth Air Force crews: "We went by passenger train to the Frankfurt on Main RR station and by streetcar to the Luftwaffe interrogation and processing center in the northwest Frankfurt suburbs. Following solitary confinement during the interrogation process, some very basic medical attention, and a one-night reunion as a crew, we were separated into officers and enlisted men." The four officers were sent to a camp at Frankfurt on Oder. The six enlisted men, including Claude, went on a long ride in an overcrowded boxcar to Stalag Luft VI. He remembers, "Arrival at the camp was a relief. Not only were the pressures and uncertainties of solitary confinement, interrogation and the train ride behind us, but we were reunited with fellow servicemen." During the days that followed, however, Claude's feelings surprised him: "I experienced the slowly dawning but shocking awareness of a loss of something I had so taken for granted, I hardly knew it existed—a sense of security."

Stalag Luft VI was well-established and already held approximately 6,000 NCOs from the various national Royal Air Forces when captured American flyers began arriving a few months before Claude got there on February 21st. By July, Russian forces were advancing from the east and all of the Americans and several hundred RAF prisoners were moved from Stalag Luft VI—first by train, then by boat across the Baltic Sea, then again by train—to Stalag Luft IV, about 120 miles NNW of Berlin, near the town of Heydekrug. Claude remembers the inhumane treatment from the Heydekrug guards: "After arrival in the village and while handcuffed in pairs, we participated in what has come to be known as the 'Heydekrug Run,' a morale-jarring incident brought about by the actions of one psychopathic German captain. It resulted in bayonet stabs and dog bites to a number of helpless prisoners, and the loss of much of our already meager personal possessions." Claude characterized this incident as a "one-time but major aberration in the heretofore fair and reasonable Luftwaffe policy concerning the handling and treatment of POWs."

The Culture of Prisons

The "obedience" experiments of Stanley Milgram in the early 1960s, replicated by other researchers over a 25-year span, provide a valuable clue to the nature of administrative decisions in virtually all prisons. Milgram's experiments were designed to determine how far supervisors (called "teachers") would go when instructed to apply an electric shock to those under their supervision (called "students"), whenever they gave an incorrect response to a question (Milgram, 1983). The imaginary voltages ranged from 15-450v, identified on the control keys as "mild" to "dangerous"; the two highest-voltage keys were marked "XXX." There was always an "experimenter" in the room with the teachers. In one variation of the experiment, the students were in another room, out of the line of sight of the teachers, the better to conceal the fact that no actual electrical shocks were being administered. In another, the teacher and student sat across from each other and the student (played by an actor) had specific instructions about how to respond to each supposed level of shock, from mild grunting to agonized screams and complaints of heart pain (www.nature.berkeley.edu).

The study's results are unsettling. Every teacher applied the electrical shocks. None stopped voluntarily before reaching 300 volts and some went as high as 450 volts. Whenever a teacher would ask an experimenter who was responsible for any physical harm that might be done to the students, the response—"I am"—assured the teachers they were off the hook. In other words, *they could simply follow orders.* Think back to the 1945-46 military tribunals conducted by the Allied forces in Nuremberg after World War II. Nazi leaders were tried for war crimes, specifically the extermination of six million Jews. The defense used by Adolph Eichmann, who arranged the transportation of Jews and others to concentration camps like Auschwitz, was, "I was only following orders." The tribunals ruled that this defense was not legitimate, but the use of it was chilling. I find it even more disturbing, based on Milgram's work in 1983, to know that the impulse to brutal behavior, in the absence of responsibility for that behavior, still lives within us.

Milgram makes it clear why guards and prison administrators objectified, and thus dehumanized, their prisoners, removing any barriers that might have mitigated cruelty. The resulting depraved behavior became the norm. There is another side to Milgram's work, however. His experiments were entirely focused on the behavior of the teachers delivering the electric shocks, not on the students receiving them. For my own part, I had spent years counseling clients who had been the object of cruel behaviors, i.e., like Milgran's students. As I interviewed survivor after survivor who had been forced into that same student role, my previous experience provided both instant recognition of the pattern and empathy for what they had gone through. During my career, I counseled many adults and children who had experienced physical and emotional abuse. The common thread among them was that each had become an object of contempt to his or her abuser.

During my interviews for this book, whenever a survivor told me a story of the cruelty that followed being objectified, I recognized that the one-on-one abusive behavior cycle I had seen so often in the privacy of my office was also present in these prison settings. My understanding of just how deep a scar such cruelty leaves allowed me to empathize with my interviewees, though I was very careful to not assume the role of therapist. In short, I was able to look behind the wall of Milgram's experiments and amplify his findings. Through this different lens, I could clearly perceive the emotional state of each survivor who spoke with me about the cruel, even gruesome treatment they had endured.

While Milgram's conclusions about the actions of authority figures, freed of any responsibility for those actions, are readily apparent in their stories about being the object of contempt, something else is there, too. Against all odds, the survivors displayed an ever-increasing ability to erect emotional barriers between fact and feeling at the time, though many of them have since waged life-long battles with PTSD. Their sense of humanity may have been threatened, but it remained largely intact. They bore the indignities, the humiliation and the cruelties with an immense inner strength that shines through each of their stories.

There was certainly no shortage of contempt from the Nazis. Alex Ehrmann was born in Czechoslovakia in 1926, and he was 12 years old when the Hungarians took over Czechoslovakia in 1938. Alex remembers that, from then on, his family's life began "a slow process of getting into hell, practically and physically." The Hungarian government was a dictatorship and they openly persecuted Jews, who were concentrated into a ghetto. Every able-bodied person was forced to work but one day each week, boys aged 12 and up were sent to a training session conducted by the military. They did drills, trained with arms, and practiced sharp-shooting.

It wasn't long before the Hungarian government introduced laws that prohibited Jews from training with arms, reasoning that they were "the enemy" and could turn on the government. They were then allowed to train with mock arms, but the weekly training session soon became just one more day of forced labor— working in the stone quarry, chopping down trees and cutting up wood in the forest, cleaning streets and clearing snow on the highways, and general work on construction of public buildings. Alex said, "This was very often was accompanied by disciplinary beatings. Little by little, they conditioned us to beatings. By the time we got to Auschwitz, we were highly used to beatings."

One morning, two gendarmes knocked on the door of Alex's home. The family was told to pack one bundle per person and get ready to be taken away. Alex remembers it this way: "So we got the most important things with us into bags or bundles. We had to collect ourselves in the synagogue by about one o'clock." From there, all the Jews were taken by train to a town about 30 kilometers away, and were told to find their own lodgings with other Jewish families while the Germans finished preparing a ghetto for them. Alex and his family moved in with a cousin until the ghetto was ready, at which point they were all concentrated into an area about six blocks square, surrounded with barbed wire. Guards were posted on the entrances and exits. They were not permitted to leave the ghetto but the Hungarians did organize one trip back to their homes to get food or any other things they wanted.

After five weeks in this ghetto, rumors about transports began. The Ehrmann family also heard a rumor that one of their uncles who had fled Slovakia was looking for them to try and rescue them from the ghetto. Unfortunately he was one day too late. Alex remembers, "So when our name came to go on transport, they told us to present ourselves in one of the local four syna-gogues. They crammed us into one building, about 4,000 people, and they locked the doors on us for the evening. And it was just plain hell. Kids were crying, hungry, sick. Old people moan-ing, and intrusion by the guards." Once it was light outside, they opened the door and let everyone out, commanding them to get into a formation of five abreast and start marching down to the railroad station.

Alex may have been only a child during WWII, but he clearly remembers details of his family arriving at Auschwitz: "There was a cattle car waiting for us there. This time the windows were barb-wired into littler windows. The train was guarded by Ger-man uniformed soldiers. We didn't know the SS yet, at that time. They loaded us onto the train, with dogs barking at us and beat-ing us, 80 or 90 people to a car. They locked the doors, padlocked it. Sealed it. We had our valuables and our bundles with us so we could sit on them. No food except what we brought with us. Two night and two days, men and women together, no sanitary provisions." The Jews were told the train was headed for southern Hungary, but on third night, they arrived in Auschwitz, Poland. "We had no idea what Auschwitz is, but when we arrived we smelled a very strange stench. And the train stopped. There was guards barking commands in German, yelling 'Aussteigen! Aus-steigen!' ('Get out! Get out!'). They opened the doors. There were fourteen guys who turned out to be Jews, Jewish prisoners who were in custody before us, getting us out of the train. They told us in Yiddish to do what we're told. Don't ask any questions. We did ask questions: 'Where are we?' 'Where are we going?' In the dis-tance we saw tall chimneys flaming at the top like the chimneys you see if you pass the refinery and see excess gas being burned off. And smell. Terrible stench. Some of the Jewish prisoners said, 'You see those chimneys? That's where you are going.'"

Everyone was put back into the five-abreast formation as they got off the train. They progressed slowly forward, moving toward a good-looking uniformed German officer, with his right arm pointing left and right. Alex said, "This was Dr. Mengele, the chief medical officer. He pointed my mother and my older sister and her baby to go to his right, and my father to his left. Two boys followed my father; two sisters followed my mother. He stopped the column and he called my father back and he told him in German, 'What did you say, old man, your occupation is?' 'Farmer,' my father said. 'Farmer.' Mengele says, 'Show me your hands.' And my father showed him his hands. And he slapped him across the face and he said, 'You liar! Go to the other side.' That was the last time I saw my father and my mother and my older sister and the baby." Alex, his brother and their two younger sisters survived.

Sonia Mentelmacher took a beating for someone else's actions just like Henry Greenbaum, whose story opened this chapter. Sonia and her fellow prisoners, who were fed barely enough to keep them alive, were forced to do hard labor from 6:00 a.m. to 6:00 p.m. each day. Between a long walk to and from the work site, Sonia's job was to dig large holes in the cold ground for storing potatoes in the winter. The preoccupation with food led to one experience that was especially traumatic for her when she was 13 years old. "A girl stole something from the kitchen, and they blamed me. They beat me so hard, you know? 'Who gave me those things that I stole?' I didn't stole nothing! I just went for some water. They put me under the shower and they were drowning me and they ripped up all the clothes and they beat me up, and they showed me what they gonna hang me that I stole those things."

Max Mentelmacher wasn't beaten, but physical punishment would have been less traumatic than what he was forced to do. When the Germans finally came to Max's small town, he was conscripted for forced labor, cutting trees for firewood, building a barracks, clearing land and working in a factory. After being marched from place to place, he ended up with seven or eight hundred other Jews crammed into a barracks, like sardines. "Anyway, in the morning they came, and we didn't expect it's gonna be like a slaughterhouse. Even worse than that. So they count ten, put them up in the back of a truck and with machine gun, "bbtttrrr," they kill ten. Get another ten out from the door, on the truck. Again, they kill them. Again, they get ten more. Again, on the truck. How many bodies can you put in two trucks? Seventy? Eighty? A hundred? Until they killed all of them? They filled up the two trucks and after this they called us down. 'Everybody down to the truck!' And we had to bury them, all the people. A lot of them while they were still alive. A lot of friends of mine. Most of them, I knew them. If it makes…. They're still alive?! What could I do?"

As mentioned before, Air Force officers in many German POW camps received relatively humane treatment, but *Steve* experienced entirely different kinds of cruelty that indicated the Nazis often ignored the Geneva Conventions.[7] When *Steve's* group of prisoners left Bonn, Germany, they were loaded into boxcars and locked up for six days with no food or water. Their train was strafed three times but they never knew if it was U.S. forces or one of the Allies. When they got to their destination, Hammelburg 13-C camp, those still alive had to take all the dead soldiers off the train.

The new camp was also the object of numerous air attacks. *Steve* told me, "During air raids and everything, they would take us to the air raid shelter. Well, we later found out that there's a law, they have to protect prisoners to a certain point. It says, during an air raid or an air raid strafing or anything, you will take the prisoners to the air raid shelter. They took us to it, but they went inside and pointed a machine gun out at you, and you stood on the outside. Because nobody said you will take the prisoners *into* the air raid shelter. It says take them *to* the air raid shelter. Everybody thought, well, if you take them to it, you'd take them in. Uh-uh. We stood on the outside. A couple of times, we seen American planes come down and they would be strafing, and they'd stop and then they'd wiggle their wings just like this (gesture), 'cause they could recognize us standing out there."

Steve told me the continuous contempt reached a new low when the Commandant's dog disappeared one day. "In Hammelburg, this German Commandant had a dog. He let that dog run all around the compound. We all knew that he was just trying us, you know. If something happened to that dog, then he could kill a bunch of us. One day, this dog come up missing. So he brought us all out into the compound, and he swore up and down that we caught his dog and we killed it and ate that dog. We didn't do nothing to that dog. We didn't. Nobody knows where the dog was." The Commandant lined up a group of U.S. soldiers and set a machine gun down near the guards. He told the Americans that the guards would shoot one of them at the end of a set interval of time until somebody told him what had happened to his dog. "So it was getting pretty close to the time they were going to shoot these guys and everybody just don't know what to do, you know. And a German guard come up running and hollering, 'They found the dog!' Well, what had happened, they build slit trenches out where you go to the bathroom. Dog fell down in the pit and he was just covered. He didn't small too good either. So they had him up there and, boy, this made the Commandant really mad. So anyway, he ordered our soup kettles out. They took the dog over, soused him up and down in our soup kettle to clean him off. Then, he said, 'Eat!' Well," he laughed, "it was the only time that the soup really tasted a little better."

Throughout my years of conducting therapy sessions, I observed a consistent emotional pattern in my clients who felt overwhelmed by the number of stressors they were facing. Almost unconsciously, their survival instincts guided them to narrow their focus to the most elemental of their stressors. That same pattern surfaced during many of my interviews with the survivors. As they dealt with the multiple stresses of mourning the loss of life as they knew it, their focus often narrowed to hunger, the most basic stressor. Frankly, I—and most people in developed countries—know very little first-hand about the kind of hunger that could take you from 170 pounds to 80 pounds while in a prison or concentration camp. Such hunger was a constant state of existence, a source of stress, and the most talked-about, thought-about concern on everyone's mind. For our survivors, food became fuel. Period. The pitiful rations became a potential death sentence of their own. And "food" became the prayer—and the scar—on every heart.

Holocaust survivor, Adrienne Krausz, was born in Cluj, Rumania in 1923 into a family of famous doctors and surgeons. She led a privileged life, sheltered from the political realities in Eastern Europe, and entered medical school to follow the family tradition. Just after she completed her first year of medical studies, World War II intervened in her life plan and Adrienne's family was concentrated into a ghetto. Her description of it is grim: "We were so isolated in the ghetto. They confiscated the radios. We had no connection with the world. We had no idea about crematories. We had no idea about gas chambers, no idea 'til we went to Auschwitz. We didn't know what the smell was like, flesh burning, and we didn't know for a few minutes what was going on. At night we saw the flames from the chimney. We know the killing is there. The people who were sent away from the ghetto in the beginning? We had no idea what happened. Nobody came back so we suspect, but we didn't know really what was going on. They tricked us with everything."

During her years in a series of concentration camps, the one constant for Adrienne was hunger. Years later, during our interview, the memory was still vivid: "We didn't have any other interest in life, just to survive and to eat. Very hungry. Very hungry. Very deep resignation to what's going to be. An empty existence." She saw no point in making any plans for the future "because in camp I didn't see any future ahead of me. I was very pessimistic about it. I was so hungry at the time that I didn't even have anything else on my mind. We were like animals."

When Adrienne faced life-threatening choices on every side, she decided to go down fighting, calculating that the chance of escaping was worth the risk. She always felt there was no future in Auschwitz and the "which cliff?" decision she made turned out

better than she could have imagined. Here is what she told me:
"So my friend Judy and I decided we wanted to smuggle ourselves
out of Auschwitz on a transport truck. Even if it meant going to
the gas chamber, was better than just staying in Auschwitz. And it
worked. To our surprise, instead of taking us to the gas chambers,
they took us to the train and they took us in cattle cars and we left
from there, out of Auschwitz."

The girls were on the train for two days and one night before they arrived in Teshau, then continued on to Ravensbrück,
where they spent two weeks without ever being assigned to a job.
Finally, they went onto another train and, three days later, arrived
in Altenburg, Germany. Adrienne told me about the big muni-
tions factory there: "Five hundred of us lived like in a prison; they
escorted us to work and escorted us back to the prison. We had
a blanket and a mattress and a cushion; in Auschwitz we slept
on the floor with just a blanket. Food was a little bit better. No
gas chamber, no crematory. Twelve-hour shifts. At Auschwitz,
the Appel was terrible thing, stand out for hours. Here, they just
counted us at the door, when we left and when we came back."

Many of the fourteen North Vietnamese prisons used to hold
American POWs were in close proximity to Hanoi. Though they
all had Vietnamese names, American prisoners immortalized
each camp with a sarcastically descriptive moniker. The nine
camps outside of Hanoi were Briarpatch (no water or electricity),
Camp Hope (full of rats but the torture was less brutal than at
other camps), Portholes (located along the southern coast with
tiny cells that looked like chicken coops), Faith (more humane
treatment, including the freedom to congregate), Farnsworth (especially brutal treatment for the officers held here; enlisted men
fared much better), Skid Row (named for its filth and poor condition; eventually used as a place of banishment for Hanoi inmates
who did not cooperate), Dogpatch (in the northwest corner of
North Vietnam; colder, damper, darker), Mountain Camp (in
rugged terrain just north of Hanoi; conditions a bit better than
other camps), and Rockpile (30 miles south of Hanoi, also more
comfortable than other facilities).

The best and the worst of all the prisons were in Hanoi. Plantation was a North Vietnamese showcase prison in the former colonial mayor's home. The worst was Alcatraz which held prisoners the North Vietnamese wanted to isolate in tiny cells sunk underground with pencil-sized holes above each door for ventilation. The Zoo had cells with no windows, but the wooden door had a little give, allowing prisoners to peek out and local livestock to peek in. Dirty Bird was located near the city's thermal power plant and generated black dust and debris; it was the only camp whose location was publicized, perhaps to discourage U.S. bombing of the area. Finally, Hoa Lo, known as the Hanoi Hilton, perhaps the most "famous" of all the North's prison camps, featured rusted shackles, ever-present rats and some of the most brutal torture of Americans in specially equipped rooms. (PBS documentary, American Experience, "Return With Honor").

On February 11, 1965, Robert "Bob" Shumaker became the second American pilot to be shot down. He had ejected from his crippled F8E Crusader jet just in time to deploy his parachute, which popped open perhaps two seconds before he hit the ground. He landed in a sitting position so his back took the impact. He sustained a compression fracture of the lower vertebra, a reality he only learned many years later, since he received virtually no medical attention from the North Vietnamese. Bob was held captive for eight years, almost all in Hoa Lo prison, which he himself christened the "Hanoi Hilton." To ensure communication while they were all separated, Bob and three other leaders created the Vietnam Tap Code (see Chapter Six for details). Over the years, it was the tap code that helped the men stay focused in the face of loud speakers on the ceiling in each cell over which the Vietnamese would broadcast Oriental music interspersed with their news reports about how many airplanes they shot down and how they were winning the war. Without the tap code to convey "real" news, Bob is convinced that more men would have been swayed to give up hope.

Through all the interrogations and torture, Bob often thought back to the not-so-helpful instructors in survival school, before he and his fellow crewmembers shipped out. His description reveals that the reality of being a POW bore little resemblance to the training: "We were taught sort of a black-and-white thing. You know, you're familiar with the Geneva Convention—name, rank, serial number. That's all we had to give. We were led to believe that, 'Hey, you just hang in there, you know. You don't give them any more than that. They may box you around a little bit but, after a while they're going to get tired and let you go off and play volleyball with the rest of the boys.' So I guess we learned it in the school of hard knocks. The first time I was tortured, they left me alone in a lot of pain and I tried to commit suicide. But then after a while you realize that it's very important to resist them. It's important not because you might give them information or something, but it's important to you because, hopefully, you're going to live another 50 years and look at yourself every morning."

It is difficult for us to imagine how Bob maintained his equilibrium under such trying circumstances. An article about him in the San Diego Evening Tribune (February 15, 1965), gives us a stark portrait: "It is one thing to stand firm for the principles of truth and honor when one is in the company of upright and honorable men. It is quite another thing—more demanding of character and fortitude—to stand by what is honest and true in the midst of one's bayonet-armed enemies." One year leading up to Christmas while everyone was still in solitary, the guards came into the courtyard with a great big canvas mailbag and dumped it out. As Bob peeked through his cell door, he could see that "it was packages from home, you know. So they'd go off to one guy's cell and then come back. And this whole process took about an hour-and-a-half or something. I was keeping track and I think there were just three cells that they hadn't visited yet. Then they took the biggest box and came right to my cell. It said 'La Jolla' on it, which is where my wife was living. So they said, 'All you have to do is sign the statement.' And I said...." Bob experienced very intense emotion at this point during our interview and never finished that sentence. Perhaps this last quote of his will help you decide whether he would have said yes or no: "What helped me more than anything to keep going and survive was my desire to come back with my head held high."

Notes

1. www.ushmm.org. Holocaust Encyclopedia. Nazi Camps.

2. The War Production Board urged citizens to save the fat that came from cooking so that it could be used for making explosives. House-wives were reminded that glycerin, made from waste fats and greases, was one of the most critical materials needed for the war effort. Three pounds of fats could provide enough glycerin to make a pound of gunpowder. Nearly 350 pounds of fat was needed to fire one shell from a 12-inch Naval gun. Until Pearl Harbor, approximately 60% of the glycerin used in the United States had been obtained from fats and oils imported from the Pacific areas, most of which were under the control of the Japanese during the war (www.daytonhistorybooks.com).

3. Adrenal secretions increase blood pressure, muscle tension and levels of alertness—the integral components of heightened awareness that allow you to assess the degree of danger present in any stressful situation.

4. Psychologists began to notice intriguing statements made by clients like, "I said to myself…." or "I thought to myself…." or "I never do anything right…." or "I could never do that." Cognitive therapy involves, first, teaching one's client to be aware of the negative patterns of his or her thinking that generate stress or depression. The next step is generating energy and interest in addressing the negativity, and then actually doing something to change it.

5. www.118trs.com/max-parnell/hell-of-ofuna

6. The official date of the founding of the US Air Force is September 18, 1947. From the time that the US military purchased its first aircraft in 1909 up to 1947, the US Air Force did not exist as a separate and independent military organization. It went through a series of designations: Aeronautical Section, Signal Corps (1909); Aviation Section, Signal Corps (1914); United States Army Air Service (1918); United States Army Air Corps (1926); United States Army Air Forces (1941). WWII illustrated the value of airpower and the need to change the basic organization of the US military forces. The result was the creation of a single Department of Defense with a strong Joint Chiefs of Staff with Army, Navy and Air Force chiefs. In 1947, President Truman signed the National Security Act which established this new defense organization, along with the creation of the US Air Force as an independent service, equal to the US Army and the US Navy. (www.af.mil)

7. Military prisoners are subject to an enemy who may or may not adhere to the terms of any of the four Geneva Conventions. The First (1864) provided for the protection of all medical facilities and personnel aiding the wounded, and gave the Red Cross international

recognition as a neutral medical group. The Second (1882) extended the protection of the First to wounded combatants at sea and shipwrecked sailors. The Third (1929) added specific protections for prisoners of war. The Fourth (1949) added protections for civilians.

Chapter Two

INTERPERSONAL RELATIONSHIPS:
I COULDN'T HAVE MADE IT WITHOUT YOU

During the Korean War, of the 75,000 United Nations and South Korean soldiers captured by Communist forces, more than 60,000 were unaccounted for; 1,200 were allowed to go home. Investigations established that several thousand American prisoners died or were executed in prisoner-of-war camps. According to the report of the Congressional Committee on Government Operations, titled "Korean War Atrocities," during the 3-year period covered by the Korean War, the North Korean and Chinese Communist armies were guilty of war crimes.[8]

Carl Cossin's memories of his Korean POW experiences affirmed the Congressional committee's findings. He told me, "In the Korean POW camp, July 1950, the stench was terrible. We slept on hardwood floors without any type of bedding, one right next to the other. Have to curl up with your heels almost touching your buttocks, one hand palm-down and the other on top of it to make a pillow. Every 45 minutes you have to turn from side to side, all night long. All odors intermingling: body lice, worms, dysentery, urine. Chinese would come in to visit and would have to put cloths over their mouths and noses. They suggested we should bathe, so the Koreans took us nine miles to the Yalu River and used sledge hammers to break holes in the ice and made us bathe; 26 men died three days later from double pneumonia. And if somebody stole something, they would put us down on our knees and pour cold water on our backs. Nobody would tell."

The Koreans' cruel refusal to allow incoming or outgoing mail affected not only Carl but his family as well. As he told me, "Never got mail under the Koreans. My mother thought for fifteen months I was missing in action and had been killed. All the years I was a POW I never got no letters. They let us write letters but none of them never went out. Once we got taken over by the Chinese, they had to turn a list over, because of the negotiations, and it showed up on the American TV, every Thursday on all the stations, of the missing in action/prisoners of war. My parents found out I was alive and that's how they knowed. Then the Chinese let us start writing home and we got letters back."

Carl had a total of nine years of Army life—five-and-a-half overseas and three-and-a-half years during wartime. Much of it was spent with his best buddy, Trent. Carl served two years in Japan, and was a combat infantry soldier in World War II in the Italian Alps. He re-enlisted and later served in Korea. His memories of the hell he describes here are so strong that he "sees" them again when he's talking about them—one of the defining symptoms of post-traumatic stress.

On the trek to the POW camp from the point of his capture, one of Carl's Korean captors subjected him to a cruel "game." He took his pistol and let Carl, whose hands were tied behind his back, watch him remove all but one bullet from the chamber. Carl then told me what came next: "After he tossed the rest of 'em out in the yard, he took the one, put it in the chamber, spun the chamber, closed it up and spun it again, and he comes up to me. Now all them soldiers agreed with him playing the Russian Roulette on me. He jammed it hard against my head. Snap! He pulls it back and spun it, and they're all still laughing. Jammed it against my head again. Snap! After he did it three times he was going to keep doing it, until he got lucky, but the other three Korean soldiers began to argue with him. And he hauled off and kicked me on the right side of my head and a hunk of hair, like this [gesture], fell off. Then he walked away."

Still on the trek to the Korean POW camp, Carl faced a firing squad. In an instant, he considered the certainty of death if he did nothing and made a "which cliff?" decision to risk an escape. As he described it, "We knew they were taking us up to the firing squad. I'm thinkin', 'How am I gonna make a break for it?' I looked ahead and off the creek you could see a blocked-off irrigation ditch near a big stream. I thought that was the spot to make a run for it." The prisoners were halted near the ditch and lined up. When the Korean firing squad lined up across from them, Carl decided it was time to act: "I started yellin', 'No! No! No!' to make a fuss. One of the firing squad soldiers began to argue with his officer. The officer in charge walked over and slapped the soldier's face over and over. He leaned away from the slaps, and fired toward us, right past the officer's right hip. He cut the throat of three of our guys, in line to my right." Carl then described the move he made as the three murdered men fell backwards: "I leaped for the ditch in a traverse run, zigzagging back and forth. The officer fired past my face with his revolver. I leaped over this bank, feet first into the water and headed for the other side. There was a slant there and I leaned and pushed with my heels until I got my chest up over the bank and then I kicked my feet up and rolled into a low spot. I seen that I was lower and I just laid there." Carl stayed put until dark, and had to listen as the Korean soldiers finished off the rest of his buddies. Before they left the area, they fired randomly into the bank behind him, but Carl could tell they didn't know exactly where he was. He made it on his own for a couple of weeks before being recaptured.

Carl's closest friend in the Army, Trent, was with him during World War II and the Korean War—ample time for Carl to appreciate the importance of interpersonal support. He said, "We was in Japan together, two years prior to the Korean War. We went through the first day of the Korean War fighting together in the same company. We went through the firing squad together. We both escaped and got recaptured. We went through the Korean Death March, and spent three years in a prisoner-of-war camp together." Carl described his relationship with Trent as a "buddyship" and was convinced it was an indispensable part of the survival process: "If you've got a buddy who can take care of you when you're down, and you can reciprocate, it makes a big difference."

The two men had stayed in touch, but hadn't seen each other in 20 years when Carl learned that Trent was dying of cancer. He made two trips to visit with Trent in the hospital, talking with Trent's family about things Trent had experienced during the wars. Carl told me, "The hospital attending staff was standing outside the door listening. Next day, when I went in to see him, they had moved him to a nicer room and had two flags on each side of the door, all from the strength of my little talk to them about what I saw him do." Carl also talked with Trent's 14-year-old granddaughter, who didn't realize she actually was describing post-traumatic stress behavior when she said to Carl, "Them stories you told, Granpa'd often started them stories but never finished them. You do. You finished the stories. Grandpa would say a few words and he would stop and just stare, like this, and not say anything more."

Carl could tell that Trent's family thought Trent was making up stories, stopping and starting like that, and that made him mad enough to write a 20-page letter: "You tell them locals that gets their war from TV, that's the way I saw Trent, the soldier, do it!" The day he got that letter, Trent showed it to two of his brothers. One brother started reading and called the other over. "Listen to this. Those two hadn't saw each other for 25 years and look here, he tells it just exactly like our brother told us. Our brother didn't make that up. He told it just exactly the way that our brother been tellin' us. Our brother really experienced those things." By the time the brothers had finished reading Carl's letter, they were in tears.

The Science of Interpersonal Support

Psychological studies have repeatedly confirmed that interpersonal support—being with others, talking with others, just knowing that others are nearby to help or simply listen—is the most effective way to deal with life stresses (DSM-IV, 1994). This reality is as relevant in our daily lives as it is in the inhumane culture of concentration camps, prisoner-of-war camps and political prisons. I learned this during my years of being a psychotherapist and I confirmed it in my conversations with former political prisoners, U.S. military personnel and Central European Jews.

In every interview, the conversations were fascinating and heart-wrenching. Each group brought widely divergent experiences to the interview process. In Holocaust camps, many people experienced the tragedy of having the very person(s) who provided them support and encouragement taken away to the gas chambers. In POW camps, the surviving members of units were reminded every day of those who had been lost. At Robben Island and in Taiwan, two men who had risked their lives in order to initiate change and obtain full freedoms for their fellow citizens were segregated both from their compatriots and from those they sought to help. The valuable role that every kind of interpersonal support played in each one's survival cannot be overstated. In every setting, fellow prisoners reached out to each other. It wasn't that strangers always became the best of friends, but just knowing that *someone* was there to talk to, to listen to, decreased their feelings of isolation and loneliness.

This chapter and the ones that follow deal with the positive coping strategies the survivors devised to manage their stress. Some were well-practiced patterns from their earlier lives. Others had never been tried before, arising out of the circumstances of the moment. In each case, the common impetus to cope grew out of the attitude that pervades virtually every interviewee's story: Don't Give Up. Whenever two or more survivors who share that attitude are able to support each other through their time as prisoners, they are living illustrations of decades of research into stress-management techniques and tools.

Because there are many facets to interpersonal support, characterizing it is difficult. Each category contains elements of every other category. In short, there are few, if any, black-and-white lines of demarcation. With that caveat, I want to focus on three particular types of interpersonal or social support: instrumental, emotional and circular. The first two can be found in standard psychological literature[9]. The third is a construct of my own and will be examined more completely in Chapter Three.

Instrumental Support

Instrumental support can best be described as the providing of practical assistance, e.g., food, water or clothing. Our survivors supported each other in this way whenever they could. Inevitably, though, there were instances that called for more comprehensive instrumental support, as in the level of care required for a fellow prisoner with catastrophic injuries.

Albert Allen found himself defending the Philippines against the Japanese. The U.S. Army was in the Philippines as a result of having won the 1898 Spanish-American War, thereby gaining sovereignty over this archipelago of more than 7,000 islands and islets, located off the southeastern coast of the Asian mainland. Along with many older Americans, Albert has vivid memories of December 7, 1941, when the Japanese attacked Pearl Harbor,

Hawaii. Unlike many of those same older Americans, however, he also has vivid memories of December 8, 1941, when Japanese troops attacked the Philippines and quickly moved in to occupy the islands. Albert told me, "We were hit eight hours after Pearl Harbor and it was very bad. In other words, we had a little Pearl Harbor of our own. They destroyed almost our whole Air Force and a lot of men were killed or wounded."

By December 22, the Japanese had landed and the U.S. and Filipino forces fought their way backwards, retreating onto the peninsula of Bataan and the island fortress of Corregidor. Five months of hell followed, fueled by the steady decline of food and ammunition and by the steady loss of life. Finally, Major General Edward King surrendered Bataan for humanitarian reasons on April 9, 1942.[10] Albert remembers the surrender: "General King got word that the Japanese had broken through a line and were slaughtering the Filipinos and Americans who were there. He went forward to the commanding officer of the Japanese forces, agreed to surrender Bataan only, nothing to do with Corregidor. So we got word to turn in our equipment and surrender, and we kind of breathed a sigh of relief."

There was, however, no relief to be had for the tens of thousands of soldiers who were surrendered to the Japanese. Albert found himself engulfed in what was to become known as the infamous Bataan Death March. The men were marched for days in the scorching heat through the Philippine jungles. Albert told me, "We only had to go seventy-five miles to Camp O'Donnell but it took us about four or five days. No water and no food. The rate of death for our people was between 45 and 50 percent." While they were moved to several different camps after O'Donnell, the inhumane treatment—insufficient food, dirty water, no medicines—was the one constant. In all, seventy-five hundred American troops were murdered or died of thirst and exhaustion during the April 1942 Death March, which followed the final surrender of the garrison at Bataan (Breuer, 2002)."

Albert's injuries at the time of the surrender were so severe that he was separated from the other Americans in the Japanese POW camp. Another prisoner, Watkey, was assigned to take care of him on a full-time basis. Albert swears he would never have survived without his caregiver. Not only was Watkey adept at dealing with Albert's physical needs but, equally important, he was another American who could speak with understanding about baseball, American cars and a host of other subjects about home, conversations that meant the world to Albert. When his legs grew stronger, Watkey was there to cheer him on through his first awkward attempts at walking. Albert remembers, "I had a real close guy that kept me alive in the hospital. I was unconscious for over three weeks, then I come to all of a sudden. Well, here sits Watkey. He kept feeding me what he could, for me being unconscious; otherwise, I'd have been dead. We talked a lot, and it would always be about home and things we would laugh about."

Years after the war, Albert finally learned why the Japanese soldiers were so contemptuous of their American prisoners of war. "Bushido" is the code of honor for samurai warriors, who would commit suicide to avoid falling into enemy hands, both to lessen their shame and to avoid possible torture. It is not surprising, then, that the Japanese combat troops in charge of U.S. prisoners treated them so badly. Albert said, "We were not brainwashed like Korean prisoners. It just was the Japanese and their sadistic ways. They weren't too happy with us at all because of their losses in the Philippines. And of course the spirit of 'bushido' states that any man that surrenders is the lowest form of life there is, so the Japanese thought we were terrible just for the fact that we had surrendered."

Bill's experience at the Viet Cong POW camp was quite similar in that a fellow soldier, Jim, was assigned as a caregiver. *Bill* enlisted in the Army two months after his 18th birthday. After basic training, he shipped out to Vietnam on January 2, 1968. He took part in patrols and search-and-destroy missions before fighting in the Tet Offensive in March 1968. *Bill* was still only 18 years old on the afternoon of May 6, 1968, when the 30 men in his company went out on patrol, close to the demilitarized zone (DMZ) on the border of North Vietnam. *Bill* was the point man, a good 20 feet ahead of the rest of the men. None of them had any idea they were walking into an ambush.

While on the top of a dike in a rice paddy, *Bill* stepped on a land mine. The explosion not only knocked him out, but also alerted the Viet Cong and a firefight broke out. Three hours later, *Bill* regained consciousness and heard the sounds of the battle. Men were yelling, screaming and shooting, all with an artillery barrage going on and planes overhead. *Bill* began to take stock of where he was and realized he must have stepped on a mine: "This thing that I stepped on was a 'Bouncing Betty.' It's called a 'junk mine' and is filled with rocks, nails, and glass. It has like four or five stages in it and every time it goes off it bounces and it keeps going up higher. After about the third or fourth time it hit, it was almost to the middle of my back and finally knocked me off the dike that holds the rice paddy, like the sidewalk. It's funny the way the thing was. It ripped the top of my boot off and got me in the foot, ankle, shin, knee. Then it hit the buttocks, crossed over and hit the other buttocks and then came down the other leg… knee, shin, ankle, foot. It took the first two toes of each foot off."

Now awake, but with no one able to help him, *Bill* tried to stand up and discovered he had no feeling from the waist down. The effort caused him to pass out again. As darkness approached, *Bill* awoke again. Things had quieted down and he now suffered the double trauma of being wounded and being left alone. Eventually he heard the voices of Vietnamese approaching, but had no idea if they were friendly or not. As they came upon him, he heard "Chu Hoi," "Surrender or die." The Vietnamese surrounded him and when he told them he was injured, they didn't believe him. Several times they tried to make him stand but he could not do it. He then felt a sharp pain and a ringing in his head. When he put a hand up to his ear, he realized they had shot him. Fortunately the bullet entered his neck and exited out his ear without doing any vital damage.

The North Vietnamese soldiers could have killed him or simply left him to die. We will never know why, but they did neither. They took the trouble to devise a rough sled on which to lay him. The back end rested on the ground. The front had handles which the soldiers used to pull the sled through a long and difficult journey to the POW camp where other American soldiers were held. For more than four years, *Bill* was transferred from one POW camp to another, first at Portholes, then "D-1", then the Rock Pile and Plantation Gardens. During that time, he remembers that he was not beaten as much as the other prisoners and thinks it was because he had become a showpiece for any visiting dignitaries. Although all the other American prisoners were in individual cells, one of them was always assigned as *Bill's* buddy—a constant companion to be with him, care for his injuries and change his dressings.

After being given basic medical instructions by the Viet Cong, Jim stuck with *Bill* through the frequent changing of dressings, administration of medications, feeding, bathing and toileting. Under such constant care, *Bill's* condition slowly improved. It took a while for him to realize his injuries were so extensive that he would always need total care from another person. As he wrestled with discouragement and self-pity about his future as a wounded veteran, Jim reacted with tough talk, guiding his buddy through those dark times. "Jim felt like a father to me. He gave me a kick in the butt, so I wouldn't feel sorry for myself!"

Finally, in January 1973, *Bill* came to the Hanoi Hilton. News about Jane Fonda coming to Vietnam as a friend of the Communists was accompanied by news of the negotiations between the two governments as well as rumors about being liberated. At the same time, food became a little more plentiful and fluctuated from the earlier diet of one bowl of rice and a cup of water to three or four bowls of rice and some bread every day. The liberation rumors turned out to be true, and *Bill* flew out of Hanoi in March 1973 on a C-31 transport. After spending a total of six months in several Army hospitals, he was discharged on September 27, 1973.[11]

Zbigniew Marian Haszlakiewicz had a whole group of caregivers. He was born in Tsarist Russia into a Catholic family that emigrated to Poland to escape the brutal Russian Revolution. With Germany invading Poland from the west and the Soviet Army moving in from the east, the entire Haszlakiewicz family faced a "which cliff?" decision. The ruthlessness of the Soviet forces was still fresh in their minds and they decided to flee to the west, toward Germany. Though they hoped that choice would give them a better chance of survival, the German occupation was harsh. Everything was forbidden for the Poles, including education, but Marian was a resourceful person. He learned about an underground school established by some professors who fled from Krakow and talked himself in. Teachers and students all knew that if the school were discovered by German authorities, the students would go to a concentration camp and the teachers would be shot on sight. Classes were held in a different house every day, with no more than nine people in any one class.

By 1943, Marian had finished high school. Almost immediately, his teachers recruited him to become one of them, and he began to teach history and physics, traveling from town to town, house to house. When he was eighteen years old, Marian was arrested as a member of the Polish Underground and held in Gestapo headquarters in Tarnow. For two weeks, he was entirely alone in a room and subjected to daily "interrogations." His main concern was with the safety of the 60 people involved in the underground school, fortunately still unknown to the authorities, and Marian kept that secret in spite of the torture to which they subjected him.[12]

After the Gestapo decided that they were not going to squeeze anything more from Marian, he was removed from solitary and transferred to a house in a town near Warsaw, into a room already occupied by eleven people. He came to this new prison with disabling injuries to both hands, inflicted intentionally during those two weeks of daily interrogations. The twelve men never discussed anything, including what had been done to Marian's hands, because it was too dangerous.[13] Marian said, "I was in such a bad physical condition that all these other people were preoccupied how to help me." He added that it was "very lucky" that the entire group became his rehabilitation team, "because otherwise I would not be able to do anything. My hands were out of order whatsoever. The real guardian angel for me was a principal in a school, very knowledgeable of people's needs, first aid, physical problems and rehabilitation. He really brought my hands back to work."

It took a long time for the caregivers to restore some of the muscles in Marian's hands. His positive attitude was a major component of the healing, and he still loves to laugh at himself. "There were occasions for laughing. For instance, when they finally restored some muscles in my hands, the first thing they let me do was to keep the spoon to eat. Somebody helped me to begin with, then later on I succeeded. And when I got the first spoon of soup to my mouth, then everybody was, you know, enthusiastic!"

Max Mentelmacher didn't need such comprehensive care, but his buddies stepped in to help with instrumental support at a critical moment. Max was just a kid during the Holocaust. He was put on a work detail with 52 other boys from his hometown, most of whom were two or three years older than he. The boys worked for a small German company, building a railroad and a truck track. Max said, "Was very hard work, very hard that you wouldn't believe it. I can't describe it, 12 hours a day, seven days a week." He tried his best, but was unable to work as hard or as long the older boys. Max then told me, "All of a sudden, one time, my foreman came up. He was German. And I was working with a shovel, you know, and he grabbed the shovel and, boom, he hit me, my left arm. See, my left arm is crooked." Once the foreman left, the older boys swung into action. Max continued: "I couldn't work, so the boys, they helped. There was no doctors, so they took some pieces of splintered wood and they splintered the arm. And they did the work, because, you know, you had to do so much every day, so they did the job for me. "

Max was on the receiving end of some openly rebellious acts on the part of local villagers. He told me, "After they divided us in different camps, I was sent away in an open cattle car. It was maybe 40 below zero, and they put 120 people in a cattle car. There was no roof, no food, nothing at all. They told us, in German, anybody who's gonna die, we have to throw it out. That was in the town of Gilvitz, and they pulled off through Czecho-slovakia. The Czech people were very good people. When they heard that a transport is coming, they came out [on bridges over the tracks] and they threw down to us pieces of bread, whatever they had. And the Nazi soldiers were shooting to them, but they kept on coming. Whoever could grab something was okay." Max traveled that way for 11 days, with devastating results. "From 120 people, we went down alive to 22 people. We were already almost dead, too."

Emotional Support

Emotional support is encouragement that makes the recipient feel cared for. Since it is virtually impossible to draw a definitive line between emotional and instrumental support, it is not surprising that the survivors offered both kinds of support to each other instinctively, whenever and however they could. For example, many Holocaust and POW camps prohibited conversations among the prisoners. While you and I take it for granted that we can talk to others any time we want to, the survivors grew to appreciate conversation as a precious experience that confirmed they were not alone in the world. It is only with immense empathy that we can begin to understand how highly they valued someone else's time and attention, when time and attention were the only things anyone could offer. It is not surprising then that these next two survivors both appreciated the value of dialogue.

Alex Ehrmann said, "The only activity we were able to do was talking to each other, recalling incidents in life, recalling family. I made a friend in Auschwitz in the next bunk, who I would meet up with about fifty years later." Joe Diamond echoed that feeling: "It was helpful to talk to others. It made you almost feel like a human being, if you could talk with people and not be alone. It can kill you, just being alone." But Joe also makes very clear that it was not always easy to offer support to someone else. He said, "Unfortunately, everybody had their own problems, especially on death marches. When people couldn't walk anymore and they were dropping, others tried to help, but not for too long, because they were so weak themselves. You can't be a hero, but if you're with people suffering, you can't just ignore, you can't just walk away. If you see somebody dying and he needs a little water, you gonna share it with him. Things like this always happened."

But circumstances weren't always so bleak. In virtually every country occupied by the Nazis, citizens engaged in covert and overt opposition. Joe was one of the beneficiaries, receiving some completely unsolicited interpersonal support that gave him hope. A woman who had been Joe's neighbor in a nearby village gave him a silent greeting in the form of a brief nod, twice each day. In the morning as Joe was marched out of the camp to go to work, and again in the evening as he returned, she and her small child stood near the camp gate. As Joe passed by her, she nodded. No words were exchanged because it was not safe to do so, but her actions provided a sorely needed boost for Joe's morale. He said, "That encounter was very helpful to 'get outside' of my own thoughts for a while. I could think about them in the village I knew so well. When that happened, a little bit of comfort would be there, and I would think to myself, 'Well, she knows I'm here.'" We do not know if this woman nodded to other prisoners as well. But we do know that she was there twice a day, no matter what, to offer this greeting to her former neighbor in a moment of quiet rebellion against the Nazis.

Stanley Wiczyk's "which cliff?" decision to go into hiding rather than wait for certain transportation to one of the Holocaust camps resulted in him receiving some life-saving emotional support. Stanley was born in 1912 into a lower-middle-class family in Poland. His early years were largely unaffected by politics but as the calendar rolled into the 1920s, Fascist parties in Poland were getting stronger and anti-Semitic activity was increasing throughout all of Eastern Europe. Jews accounted for one-third of the Polish population; the other two-thirds were evenly split between Poles and Ukrainians. Stanley went to medical school in L'Vov, located in far-western U.S.S.R. He graduated in 1938 and immediately married his fiancée who was still a med student.

Even at this early stage of war, Stanley had already come to believe that the Germans would kill all the Jews. He told me why he thought so: "There was a store. The Germans had 3500 calories a day. The Poles had 1800. The Jews had 180. So, this is impossible. We saw the line to a Jewish store where they getting their 180 calories of food. I said they were all cadavers, all would be killed. Soon. Cadavers, not people." Stanley knew he and his wife would have to fight for their lives and, even as they were finishing their educations, they began plotting how to evade the Nazis. They decided to leave L'Vov separately to increase their chances of survival. Stanley said, "Would be better if I would go first. Terrible situation. If we say to each other good-bye, we might never see us again. And my wife said, 'If you feel this way, go alone. I believe that we will meet again.' So I went and began posing as a Christian to stay alive." (The sheer luck of genetics had endowed Stanley with blond hair and blue eyes, and his mother had given him a name, Stanizlov, which was not a common Jewish first name.) His wife stayed in L'Vov to take the last two exams before getting her own medical diploma. She then went to Warsaw and got a job in the Jewish hospital there, also posing as a Christian.

As soon as he had graduated, Stanley was immediately drafted into military service. He was supposed to be honorably discharged in September of 1940, but the war started September 1, 1939, when the Germans rolled across Czechoslovakia's northern border and into southern Poland. Poland's army was no match for the Nazis and by September 18th, defeat was certain and retreat no longer possible. Early in the day, there came a general order, "Everybody on your own!" The army was unceremoniously disbanded. Stanley joined with a small group of four officers and a few enlisted men and stuck together, hiding in the woods for about two weeks. Once they had made their way back to Czestochowa in southern Poland, where they had been stationed, everyone went their own way.

Stanley's first opportunity to pose as a Christian happened on the spur of the moment. After he said goodbye to his compatriots, he met two girls passing on the street. He told them he was an officer coming back from the war, and they took him to their home so he could get cleaned up. Their father asked him if he was Jew, and he simply said, "No." After a bath, a German boy just out of high school helped him get to Warsaw. When he got out of the truck, he began to walk toward the spot where he and his wife had planned to meet if all went well. Less than five minutes later, their fears of never being reunited were put to rest as they caught sight of each other on the street.

Their Christian masquerade was certainly successful as a strategy, but it came at great cost. Stanley had found work in a clinic and he told me about a terrible dilemma he faced one day: "In this small place, the time came for the Jews to be killed. The clinic that I was running has a Jew helping. So, wife and six children. He came to me and said, 'Doctor, we Jews have to go tomorrow and to be at 6 o'clock at such-and-such a place and I will probably never come back.' The same evening, I was afraid to leave home because I couldn't picture it. What would I say if he would come say to me, 'Help me!' With the wife and six children, 'Help me!'" Stanley learned that the Germans had taken those Jews who had gathered at the 6:00 deadline to a place about five miles outside of town, and killed them all. The Germans then came back to town, looking for more Jews. "The Germans say to me, in German, 'Are there any more Jews here?' And I said in German back, 'There are no Jews here.' They were killing the remnants and we did see. I brought my wife to see the Jewish mother naked and the Jewish children naked. I didn't see the killing. I only heard the killing. It always is with me."

Another survivor, *Ginny*, was also in hiding, though the emotional support she desperately needed was scarce. *Ginny* was eleven when her parents made their "which cliff?" decision about how to protect her from the Nazis. *Ginny* was born in Paris, France, to non-observant Jewish parents. She was still living in Paris with her parents and her brother in 1939, when Germany started the attack on France. Because Paris became the main target of German air raids and bombings, the French government decided to evacuate all children from the city and sent them to refuge in the countryside. *Ginny* was sent to a summer camp in the eastern part of France; her brother was evacuated to a village in Normandy. *Ginny* remembers that she was extremely frightened to be without her family for the first time in her life.

Once the French army surrendered to Nazi Germany, the children were returned to Paris. France, itself, was split in two, with Germany occupying the north. The south, called "Vichy France," was considered "free" but was led by a puppet government controlled by Germany. In Paris, rumors were circulating about Jews being arrested and sent to concentration camps. Immediately after the German takeover of Paris in 1940, *Ginny's* mother gathered her children and escaped with them to Paulhaguet, a little village in central Vichy France where *Ginny's* father was recuperating from a disease. With the help of the village's physician and all the villagers, the family stayed there safely for several years. *Ginny* remembers that when her parents had to turn in their passports to get new ones marked with a "J" for "Jew," the village woman working in the passport office also returned their old passports to them so they would be able to identify themselves without the Jewish designation if necessary.

When the doctor and the chief of police informed *Ginny's* family that the Nazis were about to look for Jews in the local area, they decided to hide in the woods. The doctor arranged for *Ginny* to stay in Lafayette Castle, a children's hospital in the nearby mountains; her brother stayed in the boys' hospital nearby. Since *Ginny* had breathing problems, none of the employees in the hospital were suspicious. She told nobody she was Jewish and pretended to be Christian, going to mass, singing in the choir and living like a typical Catholic girl. In 1944, France was liberated by the Allies and *Ginny* was reunited with her brother and her parents. She had indeed survived the Nazis, but the public repudiation of her Jewish heritage filled her with such guilt that she still remembers feeling like a sinner every time she went to mass.

Four sets of siblings provided essential emotional support for each other. Each pair of brothers were the only surviving members of their respective families. Alex Ehrmann, Martin Weiss and Jack Gun had their older brothers with them; Curtis Brooks had his twin. The sudden loss of their parents, other siblings and extended-family members was disorienting, to say the least. Each pair of brothers was dealing with that traumatic loss as best they could, under the circumstances. All eight boys knew their parents would have wanted them to do everything they could to stay alive, stay together and care for each other. Each time they figured out how to do that was a tiny victory, a positive action they could take together that had a moment-to-moment impact on their experiences. In ordinary life situations, brothers often tease, fight and play with each other. These boys had no such luxury. Instead, their lives were intensely focused on adjusting to a new two-person family unit, finding food and staying alive however they could.

The older brothers of Alex, Martin and Jack, kids themselves, had the added burden of having to be the strong one, the brave one, assuming a parent-like role because their little brothers needed them so much. Alex said, "My brother and I never separated. He got a job in the kitchen peeling potatoes, so he was in camp when I came back from my work. I saw a gathering in one part of the camp, so I walked toward there. My brother, from a distance, yelled out, 'You don't go there! There's a selection going on.' So I disappeared. My brother, he completely understood me." Martin Weiss and his older brother entered Auschwitz when Martin was 14 years old; they were there for a year-and-a-half. He remembers holding out his hand for bread and getting a very meager portion, as well as standing outside in the cold all night for the repetitive and cruel "Appel" or roll-call. He learned to emotionally remove himself from the sight of how many dead people there were every morning. He says he wouldn't have made it without the presence of his brother, who provided what emotional support he could. Martin said, "I had an older brother who wasn't afraid of anything. I tried to emulate him."

After the U.S. and Filipino military retreat left the allied civilians in the Philippines at the mercy of the Japanese invaders, it took less than a month for the Japanese forces to capture over 5,000 civilian men, women and children—most of the Allied civilian population—and place them in internment camps. A three-year struggle for survival ensued as the internees endured crowded living conditions, disease, limited medical supplies, heavy labor, uncertainty and near-starvation.

Curtis Brooks' family was part of a wave of American immigrants to the Philippines before the war. He was thirteen years old when he and his twin brother, along with their parents and virtually all the other Americans in the islands, were concentrated into an internment camp in Manila. They lived there 37 months, battling the insufficient rations of food every single day. Curtis told me, "It was a massively disorganizing event and our lives were completely changed." Curtis' family felt no particular physical threat, but they became obsessed with food. His parents tried to supplement as best they could what the family lacked in food, but the possibilities were limited. Even so, they did everything they could to take care of each other. Curtis said, "They protected me and I protected them, but the last months of internment, we faced a terrible food shortage. Man, you went to bed hungry. You woke up hungry. You sat down at meals hungry. You got up hungry. You were always hungry. You knew that you would never be not hungry, until liberation came. It was very corrosive. *You* go without food for a while, you see how your mind focuses on that. I've never forgotten it. Perpetually hungry."

Curtis quickly learned to live in the present. Everything he saw led to a kind of shying away from trying to look too far ahead because, as Curtis put it, "it was menacing and unpredictable. You couldn't count on next week being able to do what you were do-ing this week. It made long-term planning seem frivolous. Who knows what's going to be going on?" Even after their release and return to the U.S., it took Curtis a long time to be able to depend on a predictable future. He remembers, "When we first came to this country, people would say, 'What are your plans?' We tended to not…it seemed hard to make plans 'cause you weren't used to that kind of mental activity. It was futile before, and it took a while before it seemed less futile."

Curtis and his twin brother had an advantage of sorts, in that there was a sizable group of similarly aged children in the Japa-nese internment camp. They all provided invaluable emotional support for each other. Curtis said, "I'm a twin and my brother and I were together almost constantly. It was handy to have someone same age, abilities, ideas. He was good company. Other children I'd grown up with were all at camp as well, kind of a compressed community. In a way that was a very helpful thing. School continued in camp, eighth grade to third-year high. We had important bonds of friendship and association, very strong with others besides my twin." The twins were thrown together in a room with 15 or 20 other people. Curtis remembers that most their discussions were relations of the events, discussions of the war, discussions of the events they had all witnessed, trying to interpret them. He remembers, "We were forever trying to puzzle out what the course of the war would be, because our freedom depended on it. That kind of discussion, the exchange of experiences, of ideas, was important."

The last months of internment were dramatic. There was increasing air action over Manila. "We watched Manila burn until you'd think it couldn't burn any more. Endless parade of wounded. Blood ran in the gutters. Bombs pounding night and day." The family knew at some point they would be freed but the hunger was still constant. Curtis remembers this as the toughest time, and his memories are inextricably linked to memories of his parents. His father was so determined that his children should survive that he frequently shared his food portions with them. As Curtis said, "We knew the Americans would come. It was just whether we'd be there to greet them. My dad wasn't. He starved to death a week before liberation. It came kind of fast. We were always together, but he became too weak to stand and went to the camp hospital. Died the next day. Just gave way."

Curtis' mother was determined to carry on for her twin sons in spite of the loss of her husband, but it was not to be. Liberation Day dawned with a barrage of shell fire and before it ceased, she had been killed. By the time the Americans liberated the camp, Curtis had lost both his parents and, at the age of 16, he and his twin were on their own. Those three years in the internment camp radically changed the course of Curtis' life. All these years later, he told me, "You certainly come out different. I don't know what I'd have been like if I hadn't been through the war, but you come to appreciate a number of things. One thing that I realized after I came to this country, been here a couple of years? We'd seen empires rise and fall."

While Alex, Martin and Curtis were confined in camps, five-year-old Jack and his older brother were in hiding. Jack was born in 1934 and lived in a small city in eastern Poland, which today is in the Ukraine. The majority of the 12,000 citizens were Jewish, while the surrounding farmland was mostly owned by Christians. Jack's father had a business selling fabrics, an important commodity in a setting where people used to make their own clothing. Jack had a brother ten years older who survived with him, and a sister seven years older who did not. He remembers as a little boy never being short of food and having most things that an average kid in those days would have, maybe even a little more, including bananas, oranges and grapes, which were a luxury in Eastern Europe in those years.

In short, the family lived a nice quiet life up until the chaos of World War II broke out in 1939. In September of that year, the Germans made a pact with the Russians that divided Poland in half. The Gun family was in the Russian half. In June of 1941, Hitler broke the pact and started to march eastward. Jack remembers that everything changed: "I was only seven years old when the Germans marched into our city with trucks and tanks and motorcycles. I still don't know why I was so afraid." As soon as the Germans came in, they started to harass the Jewish population. Jack said, "Not because we were bad citizens, not because we were stealing, not because we were killing, not because we were not obeying orders. Our only sin was being born Jewish."

After about eight weeks, they ordered all Jews to meet in the center of town and bring with them only what they could carry. Jack has one memory of that time, "carrying my pillow under my arm." The Germans put yellow stars on the back and front of each Jew and marched them into a ghetto, the poorest part of town with the worst housing. Jack told me, "They put three, four families in one little house and the living conditions were very, very bad. Sanitation was horrible. Food was very scarce: so many ounces of bread a day and at night, a hot cup of soup which was nothing but hot water. The old and the sick died; the younger people existed. All able-bodied people were taken to work every day, around the area, whatever chores needed to be done."

Jack's mother and sister had jobs in the laundry, washing German uniforms. His dad and brother worked on a base where the farmers used to bring goods to pay their taxes to the German government. The youngest children stayed in their communal house with an older woman to look after them. Jack said, "We were afraid to go outside, because we used to look out the window and see a lot of horrors. Hitting people with the rifle, with the butt of a rifle for no reason at all. Kicking people. Shooting people."

In Warsaw, before the Germans came in and concentrated all the Jews into a ghetto, Jack's father had given the family's valuables to a farmer who was a trusted family friend, a Christian Czech. That man risked everything over the course of four years to provide instrumental and emotional support to Jack and his older brother. After about a year in the ghetto, rumors started that the ghetto was going to be liquidated, but nobody really knew what was going to happen. Jack's father made a plan to sneak Jack out of the ghetto with him and his older brother when they went to work. He would hide Jack during the day, then the three of them would meet and run away to the Czech farmer, hoping that he would hide them. The sneaking-out and the hiding worked as planned. However, during that day, Jack's father learned that his wife and daughter had been kept from going to work, an indication that their work was no longer needed and they would be killed. At the end of the workday, he brought Jack's older brother to the haystacks in the barn where Jack was hiding and told the two boys to spend the night there. He planned to go back to the ghetto, assure himself of the safety of the women, and then return the next morning for the escape attempt with his sons.

Jack's father never came back. The boys knew something happened but didn't know what, so they continued lying there in the hay. A couple hours of later some German soldiers came in, screaming, "Any Jews? Any Jews come on out!" They poked into the hay with bayonets, but never reached either brother. The boys stayed there, not making a sound, for the whole day. When it got pitch black outside, they sneaked out of their original hiding place and spent the next night in the hayloft of another barn. When that farmer came to do his chores the next morning, he heard some movement from the hayloft and climbed up to find the two Jewish boys there. He told them what had happened the day before to the people in their ghetto: "They took everyone out about 15 miles outside of town and killed all 4,500 of them. Whoever didn't die with a bullet died from suffocation." For the boys, that meant they had lost not only their parents and their sister, but 20 or 25 aunts, uncles and cousins. The farmer then told the boys about a new German law, that if they found a Christian holding a Jew on his property, they would kill the Christian and his family, the same as the Jew. He said he would give them bread and water, but they would have to leave once it got dark.

Jack's brother knew where the Christian Czech farmer lived and somehow, some way, got the two of them to this farm. They knocked on one of the windows and woke him up. The first thing he did was make the sign of the cross, because he knew what had happened in the village and thought the boys had come back from the dead. Jack said, "My brother told him how we got away, and he says to us, 'I promised your father that I would help him or anyone from his family that needed help. I'll do my best, but I cannot keep you on my property. For now, the wheat is still high. You go out and lay in the wheat all day. At night, I'll come out and bring you some food. Every few nights, you can come into my barn. I'll feed you, but we cannot make it look obvious because we don't know who we can trust.' Those people were really, really righteous people. They were like angels."

For the next two years, the boys lived in the woods when the weather was warm. They joined forces with a man and his daughter and the group of four spent that first winter in a hole dug into the ground with a door on top. The next winter they were taken to a safe house way out in the country. Their area was liberated in April 1944, a year before the war was over elsewhere. Jack told me, "We all went back into our old house after the Germans fled. For two more years, the same farmer used to still give us food. We were hoping maybe somebody else from our family ran away or something, you know what I mean? Maybe, you know, when you don't see with your own eyes them getting killed, you hope. But there was nobody." Trying to put their lives back together, the four spent two additional years in a displaced persons' camp in Linz, Austria, getting packages of food from the United Nations. During that time, Jack turned 11 years old and, for the first time in his life, went to school. Jack's brother eventually married the girl who had hidden with them all that time and, in January 1948, they all emigrated to the United States.

The second of the three former political prisoners I interviewed took immense risks to further the work of helping his country throw off the oppression of apartheid. Ahmed Kathrada was one of Nelson Mandela's close compatriots in the African National Congress (ANC), which had been banned by the South African government in 1960. The inner circle of Mandela supporters were supported and encouraged by countless "foot soldiers" in their battle against apartheid. The repressive South African government had routinely abused, tortured and murdered dissidents, even forcing some to jump to their deaths from a tall building in Johannesburg. "You see, what happened in South Africa was, there was a law that allowed the security police to detain suspects for purposes of interrogation to extract information. Now, suspects were kept completely incommunicado, alone. No lawyers, no visits, we were not even allowed to talk with our colleagues with whom we had been arrested (Kathrada, 2001)."

The ANC leaders, including Mandela and Kathrada, were tried at the Rivonia Trial, which lasted from October 1963 to June 1964. Though they had feared the death penalty, all the activists were instead found guilty of sabotage and, on June 12, 1964, were sentenced to life in prison. They were confined in Robben Island Prison, situated on a small rocky islet about seven miles off the coast of South Africa near Johannesburg. (Starting near the end of the 17th century, Robben Island was used to isolate various groups of people, including lepers, until 1931. From 1962-1989, large numbers of political activists were incarcerated there.) Kathrada served 18 years on Robben Island before being transferred to Pollsmeer Maximum Prison, near Cape Town. All the while, Kathrada wrote copiously in prison; a book, *Letters From Robben Island,* grew out of those long years. In the book, Kathrada cites a poem by Jan F.D. Cilliers, a noted Afrikaaner poet, the silent repetition of which had sustained him throughout his adult life. The poet praises a person who, in the face of adversity, can hold his own. During his trial, Kathrada, who felt the poem would prove valuable to the interrogation, recited it to one of his interrogators in the original Africaans (Kathrada, 2001).

Ek hou van 'n man wat sy man kan st
Ek hou van 'n arm wat 'n slag kan slaan
'n Oog wat nie wyk, wat 'n bars kan kyk
En 'n wil wat so vas soos n' klipsteen staan.

I like a man who stands as a man
I like an arm that can strike a blow
An eye that never shies away, that can pierce a crack
And a will that stands steadfast as a rock.

The longer two men share the experience of being imprisoned, the stronger the resulting "buddyship," to quote Carl Cossin. Ahmed Kathrada and his friend, Lalo, were captives of the South African government for more than 20 years. Through it all, they supported and encouraged each other: "I think that beyond the individual level, prison cements friendship. My friend here who is with me [at Chautauqua, where I interviewed him], we developed a very close friendship, closer than between me and my own brothers. I knew him before, but it developed much more in prison. So today, he is my confidant. We discuss all kinds of intimacy, which I don't do with my family. Unlike the people outside of this, we faced Apartheid 24 hours a day. We were 24 hours under surveillance, night and day. The lights never switched off. There was a guard walking up and down the whole night, so we had to keep strong. We had to, to boost each other's morale. We had to."

The ban on the ANC was lifted in February 1990 and Kathrada was released in October of that same year, after serving more than 26 years. Imagine the stresses associated with such long incarceration, especially one that came from a trumped-up, politically motivated charge and conviction. When we factor in the isolation, inadequate food and a seemingly endless parade of days to be filled, it is impressive that these political activists proved themselves to be strong, patient, dedicated men. They used their individual and collective creativity, energy and intelligence to maintain their mental equilibrium. The anti-apartheid movement may have been deprived of their physical presence for all those years, but their value as leaders and figureheads never diminished. With the ruling that abolished apartheid, they came out of prison as heroes and stepped back into their public political lives. On the other hand, stepping back into their personal lives and reestablishing relationships with their families proved much more difficult. An entire generation of family life had been lived without them. Some parents and other relatives had died, they were strangers to their wives, and some of their children who had been babies in 1964 had babies of their own by 1990.

Larry Bott, who was born in Columbus, Ohio on December 23, 1924, had two supportive friends to help him through World War II. The Army wanted all the eligible high-school seniors in January 1943 but the principal of Larry's school refused to let them go until they had graduated in the spring. Larry actually graduated "on furlough" so the Army could get him and his class-mates a couple of weeks early. While his poor eyesight meant he would never go overseas as a soldier, he was able to be trained as a medic to fill vacancies in the U.S. forces. He spent a year in the base hospital at Fort Benjamin Harrison in Indianapolis, and was then told he would be assigned to a hospital ship.

It didn't quite turn out that way. Larry told me, "Unfortunately for me, by the time I got to Africa, I found out that all the plush jobs were taken and that I was left with only the most undesir-able jobs, like first-aid in a rifle company." On the voyage to Africa, Larry became fast friends with another recruit, Erick, also a replacement medic. When the time came for the men to be shipped out to join a fighting unit, Erick left first, assigned to the 3rd Division. Five days later, Larry was also assigned to the 3rd Division and was eager to reconnect with his friend. He told me, "I contacted the division mail clerk and asked him where Erick was assigned. He had a list of personnel and all he could show me was Erick's name with a line through it and the letters KIA next to it." It turned out that Larry had been assigned to I Company, 2nd Platoon, not to join Erick there, but to replace him.

Larry's new platoon leader, buddy, role model and mentor was Sgt. Dunham. Larry remembers him as "one of the greatest soldiers and leaders I was ever to meet in my life." Everyone in the company modeled their behavior after Sgt. Dunham: "During any attack, we always watched to see what he was doing. If he was attacking, then we attacked. If he was ducking or digging in, then that's what we did. His ability to lead was the reason we were an effective fighting unit and also the reason most of us survived the war at all."

Larry gave me a vivid account of stress under combat conditions. "All day long, you'd hear machine guns and shells going off, explosions of tanks and tanks firing, and artillery flying over the top of your head, going this way and that way. You never knew 24 hours a day whether you were going to be hit by something. And you had a lot of near-misses where you could actually see the bullets going at you. You felt it hit right by your feet. Before I was 20 years old, I was to learn such things as the difference in the sound between incoming and outgoing artillery, the paralyzing fear while advancing under fire; the crack and whine of a sniper's rifle, the smell of burning and rotting people and animals, and the blood-curdling command to 'fix bayonets.' It is one thing to fight a war when everyone stays a respectable distance and shoots at each other without seeing their faces. But to get close enough to stick each other with bayonets is enough to make you puke."

Larry got tonsillitis in December 1944 and was sent to a field hospital, where he stayed until January 6, 1945. That day, the hospital medical officer asked him if he was ready to return to the front. Larry responded that he was a soldier who "took orders but volunteered for nothing." The medical officer changed his question to an order, and Larry was sent back to I Company. Larry and the rest of the survivors in I Company were finally captured by the Germans on December 22, 1944. After being held for 4-1/2 months, they were liberated in April 1945.

Charles Brutza also experienced the stresses of face-to-face combat and the relief of some vital interpersonal support. He had just graduated from high school in New York when he was drafted at age 17. After the Pearl Harbor attack, the Army was under pressure to produce a fighting force literally overnight. Chuck remembers that his training was minimal, i.e., they gave him a gun and said, "Here's what you do: shoot him before he shoots you." After his initial "What the hell?!" reaction, Chuck became a good rifleman and he bonded with the other raw recruits in the 45th Infantry Division. Under the pressures of battle, "buddyships" were vital: "I valued talking with my buddy, because we were both in the same niche, you know? There wasn't anything he could do.

There wasn't anything I could do. But we still helped each other in that sense."

Though some POW camps, especially those for officers, offered a few privileges to the prisoners, Holocaust camps were uniformly harsh. Even so, there were occasional opportunities for prisoners to sing or talk quietly together at night, after the guards had left at the end of their shifts. In those situations, the value of inter-personal emotional support was clear, even though those pres-ent were physically and emotionally exhausted and often ill. Joe Diamond was one of the many survivors who took comfort from the night singing. He remembered, "At night, especially when we were on the bunks, sometimes we used to sing a little. It was help-ful, one more little thing that made you not feel alone."

In addition to the night singing, after-hours conversations were common. *Bob* was drafted into the Army before he finished his studies at Ohio State University, where he was majoring in poultry for a degree in agriculture. He participated in the D-Day Normandy landings on June 6, 1944. Five beaches on the north-ern coast of France were designated landing sites for invading Allied troops. *Bob's* regiment landed on Utah Beach, the west-ernmost of the five. Currents pushed their landing craft 2,000 feet west of the original target, taking them largely out of harm's way. Unlike the other four landing groups, 99% of the men who landed on Utah beach survived. *Bob* was still only 21 years old when he was captured. He ended up in a camp with 1,275 other non-commissioned officers (NCOs) and, as was nearly always the case with POW's, hunger became the primary issue. Each day they got one piece of black "jerry bread" [sic] to split between five people, a little sassafras tea and some soup. *Bob* told me, "I remember one time, there were a bunch of worms in it. That's all right…that's meat. Don't kid yourself. When you're hungry, you eat it." In his brief time there, *Bob* lost 85 pounds.

In his after hour-conversations, *Bob* loved to tell fellow prison-ers about his adventures as a chicken farmer in Ohio, an activity that was an important part of his former life. In the process of rekindling of those vivid memories, he used every possible tool—

images, words, feelings, sounds—to create a moment of sanctuary. He told me, "One of the things we used to do, they'd turn the lights off early naturally, and we'd talk about something, anything. I talked about poultry because I know my subject. After the war, we had a reunion out in Tucson and this guy says, 'I remember you. Know why I remember you? Because you talked about chickens. I learned more about chickens than I ever knew!'"

Neal Harrington's support team also dates back to the war. He has a long history as a staunch member and supporter of the American Defenders of Bataan & Corregidor, Inc. He was especially active in recruiting veterans to attend "the ultimate World War II reunion" in July 2003. The event had been planned to coincide with the official dedication of the Robert J. Dole Institute of Politics in Lawrence, Kansas. In his own post-war life, Bob volunteers at the Washington, D.C. Veterans Hospital. He also identifies and locates veterans around the country, and organizes reunions to bring them together for shared support. He said, "Four of us started these reunions strictly because I've had so many men that always felt they were the only people who had any problems. I've had a lot of people tell me, 'Are we glad you started this up! We never knew what was going on, or we always felt that we were the only people that have troubles and everything else.' We also made a connection with a guy in Florida who has helped several get their 100% disability."

Notes

8.   U.S. Congress. Senate. Subcommittee to Investigate the Administration of the Internal Security Act and Other Internal Security Laws of the Committee on the Judiciary. Communist Treatment of Prisoners of War. A Historical Survey. 92 Cong., second sess. U.S. Government Printing Office, 1972. Pp. 12-13.

9.   The John D. and Katherine T. MacArthur Foundation. Research Network on SES & Health. www.macses.ucsf.edu/research/psychosocial/socsupp.php. Social support refers to the various types of support that people receive from others and is generally classified into two major categories: emotional and instrumental.

10.   Lieutenant General Jonathan Wainwright did the same for Corregidor and the entire Philippine archipelago on May 5, 1942.

11.   Cleveland Plain Dealer, Wednesday, May 13, 1998.

12.   Sarasota Herald Tribune, October 2, 2003.

13. When I interviewed him in 2003, Marian did not give me any details of the cruel treatment, simply saying there were "severe injuries" to his hands. All these years later, those hands could still tell his story.

Chapter Three

INTRAPERSONAL SUPPORT:
MAINTAINING A POSITIVE ATTITUDE

My years of work helping clients develop some pivotal intrapersonal skills took an unexpected turn early in 1992. A close friend,
Judith Thornberry Thomas, who knew my fascination with stress
and stress management, told me about a Taiwanese political pris-
oner she had met in the late 1960s. Judith and her then-husband,
Milo Thornberry, had arrived in Taiwan early in 1966 as United
Methodist missionaries to teach in a theological college in Taipei.
They had been taught the basic history of the island: the Chinese
hand-over of Taiwan (also known as Formosa) to Japan in 1895
after their defeat in the Sino-Japanese War; the Allied return of
Taiwan to China in 1945 with Japan's defeat at the end of World
War II; and the Chinese Nationalist Army's retreat in 1949 after
their loss to the Chinese Communists. By the time Judith and
Milo took up residence there, the government was a virtual
dictatorship under the Kuomintang (KMT) Party, led by Chiang
Kai-shek. Military law trumped democratic order, and an extensive network of military and secret police vigorously suppressed
all dissent.

Within a year of their arrival, the Thornberrys had become
friends with Dr. Peng Ming-min (pronounced "Pung"), an inter-
nationally recognized professor of political science at the National University of Taiwan. If Peng had been willing to collaborate
with the repressive KMT regime, he might well have ended up
president of Taiwan. But restoring Formosa as an independent
political entity was the passion of his life. He became a "Free
Formosa" activist, earning worldwide respect for his work. Peng
and two of his graduate students were in the process of finaliz-
ing, publishing and planning to distribute a manifesto they had
written, the *Declaration of Formosa*. The document called for a
debate on the legitimacy of a government that controlled only
Taiwan yet claimed to represent the entire Chinese mainland, and
used this claim to justify denial of democracy and the repression
of civil dissent. It further called for the replacement of the KMT

regime with a democratically elected government. Since Peng
had already been branded an enemy of the KMT, the fledgling
Declaration led to immediate action by the state police. Peng was
arrested in 1964, tried in a secret military trial, and sentenced
to eight years in prison for the crime of sedition. International
colleagues, including Dr. Henry Kissinger, then a professor at
Harvard University, loudly protested his arrest and sentencing.
The combined weight of all the worldwide protests played a big
part in Peng being released from prison after less than two years
and, instead, ordered to spend the rest of his life under house arrest with 24-hour police surveillance.

Peng quickly mastered the art of slipping in and out of his
house without alerting his jailors. Even so, his ability to be a
productive leader was severely compromised. After several years
of this bleak existence, he decided it was too dangerous for him to
remain in Taiwan. He told me, "I was under surveillance for five
years before I left. They watch you until you die. Could be fifty
years, forty years. Also, I feared my life was in danger. That kind
of life is not worth living." Peng entrusted the Thornberrys with
devising an escape plot for him and, after six months of prepara-
tions, it was finally time to go. The day before he was to leave, he
took some flowers to his father's grave and then went to visit his
mother: He told me, "Couldn't tell her it was the last time, but she
sensed something. She lectured me about not going to church.
I eventually figured out that she thought I was going to commit
suicide. She sensed that I was saying goodbye. She knew I had
been under surveillance for five years and had no hope of getting
out of that."

The escape took place in January 1970, when Peng left Taiwan
right under the noses of his jailers, dressed as a tourist and traveling on a fake Japanese passport. The Thornberry's plan for him
had worked flawlessly, but Judith and Milo soon found themselves under the KMT microscope. They were arrested in March
1971, only three months after Peng fled the country, and accused
of "unfriendly activities and attitudes against the Republic of
China." After being variously labeled CIA operatives and dangerous agitators, they were deported from Taiwan only three days
after their arrest.[14] In 1992, when Judith told me she was still in

contact with Peng, who was then living in Oregon, I asked for
an introduction, hoping to explore how he had dealt with stress,
change and loss stemming from each type of imprisonment.
Judith and I met with him in Los Angeles in October of that year,
just before he was going to return to Taiwan for the first time in
twenty years, his arrest warrant finally having been lifted.

During our conversation, I discovered that Peng embodies the
most important characteristics of intrapersonal support. Always
a leader, he understood how that set him apart, pushing him to
depend only on himself before, during and after his exile. He
learned to recognize and rely on his own strengths. He used positive self-talk to fuel a positive attitude, and then used both skills
to come through his odyssey stronger than ever. In fact, only
four years after his homecoming in 1992, he was the presidential
nominee of the opposition Democratic Progressive Party (DPP)
in the 1996 elections.

Attitude: The Key to Intrapersonal Support

Our survivors augmented the pivotal skills of giving and receiving interpersonal support with their intrapersonal support skills.
Perhaps the most valuable of those skills is the development and
constant nurturing of a positive attitude. This process is not linear
and its component parts have, well, mushy boundaries with each
other. (If they didn't, psychotherapy as a career would disappear.)
A positive attitude is best achieved by perfecting three intrapersonal skills in particular: focusing on replacing negative self-talk
and with positive self-talk, creating safe zones, and recognizing
your own strengths.

We all fight a daily battle between positive and negative self-
talk. In fact, most of us tell ourselves three negative things for
each positive one (Helmstetter, 1991). Given that fact, it is striking to realize that my interviewees didn't do that. Long before
there was research data about how this works, they instinctively
knew that the way they talked to themselves could affect their
energy, their stress levels and their will to survive. They knew that
negative self-talk could close their minds to possibilities by leading them to focus on worst-case scenarios instead of best-case
ones, thereby convincing themselves that there were no solutions.

In fact, since self-talk has a way of becoming self-fulfilling prophecy, unbridled negative thinking can spell trouble. [15] Positive self-talk, on the other hand, has its roots in cognitive therapy, where your beliefs and thoughts, as represented by words and assumptions, have the greatest impact on emotions, behavior and state of mind. [16] Such beliefs have a powerful impact on your emotional well-bring and motivation. [17] They can also boost your confidence, a key to maintaining a positive attitude.

Alfred Tibor was born in Konyar, Hungary in 1920. He was able to complete his schooling at the Industrial Art & Design School in Budapest before his family was directly subjected to Nazi brutality. Alfred was drafted into the Hungarian Army in 1940 and remembers it as simply a forced-labor battalion, a "hatred action to us, to do work what machinery or animals couldn't do." In 1942, when he was serving on the Eastern Front near Russia, the Russians tried to recruit Hungarian soldiers over to their side, saying, "Jews, come over. Here you are going to be equal." In January 1943, when the Russians captured the Hungarian soldiers and they became prisoners of war, they found that "equal" in the Russians' eyes meant being equated with the Nazis.

Alfred survived the inhumanity of five-and-a-half years in Siberia. During our interview, he offered virtually no details of that time, simply saying, "I don't want to talk about too much about that. If you would read the book of Solzhenitsyn, One Day of Ivan Danulavich [sic], you would know that one day of his was also one day mine." He did say one thing, however, that gives us a clue to how he survived: "When you are lower than the snake belly, when you are worth less than a penny in your life, that's when you have to think positive. I wouldn't be here if I wouldn't think positive."

When Alfred was captured by the Russians, he and the other prisoners were forced to march for five days and four nights on the snowfield, with no food, no drink, no nothing. Anyone who sat down in the cold fell asleep and then froze to death. Anyone who couldn't keep up and fell to the back end of the column of prisoners was shot. Alfred said, "So it was with one of my comrades who wanted to sit down for a minute. And I didn't let him to sit down, because it would be a sure thing he's going to be dead. So I grabbed him in my shoulder and I carried him almost a day in my shoulder. It is about will-power, what is this mean. Even today, it is hard for me to believe I was able to carry in the snowfield almost a day my comrade, and how I get the strength."

Alfred remembers clearly that when the circumstances were so desperate, he found within himself a certain power he had never had before: "...a power which never comes from you in a normal situation. In a normal situation, I wouldn't have the power to carry another person in my shoulder. And I was one of the first ones who was walking on the snowfield. I was going up toward the leading officer, the guardian of us. I was following him, because I had then in my mind I had to be the first one, because if you are going into the crowd, you are losing that will-power. You are losing in the crowd, you are staying farther and farther back. So that was in my mind: 'I have to be the first one.' And I was going in his steps into the snow."

Life for Alfred since World War II has been focused on keeping the memory of his experiences during the war alive through sculptured pieces. He continued his interrupted art education at the University of Miami, Dade Junior College (Florida), and Columbus (Ohio) College of Art & Design. He believes his life was spared so he could do this work. Implicit in every piece is his conviction that there is beauty and value to be found in all lives. In short, for this man who has been through so much, life is still a celebration. Each time one of his sculptures is installed somewhere, Alfred's journey and his power as an artist are affirmed. [18] One sculpture in particular, titled *Ultimate Friendship*, grew out of Alfred's heroic offering of instrumental support to a fellow prisoner during the war.

In 1947, Alfred was finally able to return to Budapest, only to discover that virtually all his family had been obliterated. Determined to start over, he eventually married and began a family. In 1956, chafing under Communist rule, he elected to escape to the West with his wife and two small children. They arrived in the U.S. on January 30, 1957, penniless but free. That particular date also marks a conscious decision to change his thinking: "I stop the hatred what I went through from my birth, which was February 10, 1920, and lived with up until January 30, 1957, when I came to this country. Before, I hated so much I was dreaming in Russia I am going back to Hungary on top of a tank, a machine gun in my hand. Instead of greeting people, I am going to shoot them. But on August 11, 1947, I found out I lost everybody—my father, my grandfathers, actually 37 people in my immediate family. And that was the time I said to myself, 'I can't go down to their level. If I am going to do the same thing they did for me, the hatred is going to go on because hatred is just like a circle. The next generation is going to hate *my* action and, in that case, *I* am continuing the hatred. I am still making person responsible what they did, only I am not blaming today's generation for the fathers or the grandfathers what they did against the human race.'" Alfred is convinced he survived so he could help stop the hate. He talks to students and tells them that, even jokingly, they should never say, "I hate you!"

Safe Zones

Intrapersonal support has multiple facets. Positive self-talk and positive thoughts can go beyond words into a self-created montage of memories and visual images that can influence your mood, raise your confidence level and fuel your courage. The resulting "safe zone" is a unique virtual shelter, constructed on whatever foundation has been the solid ground under your feet for much of your life. *Harry* and *Ann* built their safe zones on strongly held beliefs. *Harry* boiled it down to ten words: "I just believed nothing was going to happen to me." *Ann* only needed nine words: "Something in my heart always said, 'You'll pull through.'"

Henry Greenbaum took refuge in dreams: "The only thing I cannot understand, when I was in there, I was dreaming all the time about my father and my mother. All the time, my father and my mother...." Even a non-therapist could easily conclude that Henry's dream was a natural safe zone for a little boy alone in a concentration camp. Albert Allen and *Vic* wrapped themselves in memories of home, particularly memories related to food. Albert remembers that, "come Thanksgiving, oh my God, the guys would sit down and they would write menus that long, you know, and start it off with this and that. I used to read them. They just... you just get...your mouth is watering." Paul, who died before the research for this book was begun, is included here because his sister, Joyce, generously shared his wartime diary with me. Joyce told me she especially enjoyed Paul's detailed lists of his favorite foods. "Pies—apple, cherry, pumpkin, peach, coconut cream, lemon. Cakes—chocolate, angel food, yellow, upside-down cake. Cereals—Wheaties, Rice Krispies, corn flakes, bran flakes, shredded wheat."

Bill's safe zone was grounded in patriotism and thinking about anything to do with America: "Saying the Pledge of Allegiance or singing 'America,' real soft to yourself, would make you feel good. And you could think about things you did, the last things you did with your family back in America, before you came over." Joe Diamond used the power of music to transport himself to another place: "Singing some of the songs we used to sing at home. It had to do with remembering. To remember families, you know? Somebody. Some ancient Jewish songs was given down from great-great-grandparents, so we tried to sing those songs, more or less to remember the family. It was wonderful." Henry Greenbaum helped me to understand that the children often could be comforted by the singing as they watched the adults reach back into their memories for songs they learned as children. Henry told me, "Thinking about my family, emotions, believing in God, humming songs to myself. Humming and humming and humming." *Hans* used his hands to create a safe zone: "I think my drawing helped. I had a rather rich fantasy life. One thing you do in a situation like that is to fantasize a lot about what's lacking."

Finally, there are safe zones that require focused mental exercises. Dick Mann told me, "I tried to do simple things like try to name every automobile that was ever made, like a Healey, Auburn...you'd go way back. The good thing about that was I'd never finish it. Out of a clear blue sky, another one would come to me and that means I had it to think about all over again." Bob Shumaker said, "I grew up in a nice little town. I would recreate the streets and the experiences I had with people there in

Granville, Ohio. I think you can understand why it's helpful to lose yourself in the skills and interests that you had before the war." Even years after escaping from house arrest in Taiwan, Peng Ming-Min told me he still took refuge in solitude. "I had a small cottage in Kansas and spent time there alone. Sometimes I didn't use my voice for a month, and I really enjoyed that time. I read everything. I don't feel alone at all when I'm by myself. I became eccentric, learned to become my own companion. I created my own universe, my own world. I went inward."

Recognizing Your Own Strengths

The survivors augmented sheer luck with courage, ingenuity and perseverance. Recognizing your own inner strengths, the third of the commonly used intrapersonal-support strategies, is fueled by that same courage, ingenuity and perseverance. When it all comes together, the result is an iron-clad conviction that, against all odds, survival is possible. The most common way to verbalize that conviction was also the simplest: "Don't give up."

Those three words embody everything. The survivors were strong and smart. They made good choices. They acknowledged their circumstances, but also recognized their inner strengths in the face of those circumstances. As they encouraged others to deal with the realities of their own situations, they realized that each time they said out loud, "Don't give up," they were confirming their own decision to persevere. Judith Altmann said, "The person that committed these crimes I cannot reach and to carry hate in me is destroying me. I'm not going to do it." *Bill* said, "We'd say we have got to make it through. It didn't matter if we were going to be there two years or ten years. We were going to make it." Bob Shumaker said, "We'd see by the pattern that the interrogations were marching down the row, that my number was coming up and you know I would condition myself by saying, 'Hey I'm going to take a bunch of heavy punishment. I'm not going to allow them to kill me.'" Thaddeus Stabholz said, "I wanted to survive Hitler and see what the world would be like after Hitler." Bob said, "I always told myself, 'They're not going to kill me if I can help it. I'm not gonna let 'em.' Not that they couldn't but I wasn't going to do anything to give them a reason to do it."

Joe Diamond said, "This is what we're going through now. It won't last forever."

Michael Stroff, who was born and raised in Florida, paid for his own flying lessons as a teenager. He had been a Navy pilot for 28 years before being downed in 1944 over occupied France. His B-17 had suffered serious damage in an air battle, and from the pilot's seat he was doing all he could to make the coastline before instructing the crew to abandon ship. When the clouds below him cleared, Michael saw that he would indeed reach land, giving his crew their best chance of survival.

All ten members of Michael's flight crew survived the bailout and were captured by the Germans. Nearing the end of 1944, France was overrun with prisoners of war and conditions in the POW camps there were very bad. Eight of the crewman eventually ended up in Stalag Luft I, while two escaped en route. Michael was part of a large group of prisoners being transported by train to Stalag Luft l when a murmur started through the train that a small group was trying to make an escape. Michael told me that was when he made his own "which cliff?" decision to stay on the train. He remembers, "The train had barred windows, and word went around from man to man, 'Anybody got a hack-saw from their escape-and-evasion kit?'" Michael didn't find out what had happened until the train arrived at Stalag Luft I. When the German guards on the train counted their prisoners, they discovered that they were 19 prisoners short. Michael clearly remembers "watching the Nazi officer in charge when the guard from the train told him. I actually saw the hair on the back of his neck bristle."

At Stalag Luft I, Michael quickly realized he and his fellow prisoners would benefit from the common practice in wartime for officers to have separate prisoner-of-war facilities from the enlisted men. Unlike like circumstances at most other camps, the prison administrators of Stalag Luft I lived up to the Geneva Convention during the 18 months Michael spent there. The POWs received parcels sent by the U.S. and Canadian governments, with the only rule being that canned foods had to be eaten right away to prevent stockpiling. He also remembers that their main food item was rutabagas, "*tons* of rutabagas, which didn't even have nutrition to recommend them." He also learned to play bridge, and loved how it kept his mind occupied. Others occupied themselves by digging tunnels and Michael remembers over one hundred of them during his 18 months there. When the war was declared over, the German officers turned the camp over to the U.S. officers. Prisoners became administrators, and the camp continued to operate as usual. Almost all the former prisoners stayed in camp and watched as 200-300 men took their chances and left on their own. Two days later, a B-17 landed, left its engines running and began to take out about 25 men at a time.

The three coping mechanisms described above are not islands, each functioning independently of the other two. In fact, they often function together, increasing their overall effectiveness. Murray Ebner's story clearly illustrates how interpersonal support, positive self-talk and recognizing your own inner strengths can work together throughout the process of survival. Murray was just a child when the Ebner family was transported to what his parents referred to as "prison camp." At the selection table, he and his parents were directed to different groups. Murray had no idea what that separation meant for his parents. He just knew that he never saw them again. One of Murray's safe zones came directly from his mother: "Believe it or not, sometimes I tried to sing the Polish Anthem. Even to this day, I can sing to you the Polish Anthem. My mother, we used to go around and walk around and sing, so I sort of repeated what she did."

He told me, "Once, somebody asked me, 'Did you ever think about committing suicide?' I said, 'Absolutely not.' I never thought about committing suicide because, first of all, I didn't know anything about suicide, and second, I was hoping my parents were waiting for me. I thought, 'Sure, I'm strong enough. I can take care of it. I'll survive.' I just tried to grow up. Just tried to grow up. I was thinking all the time, worrying that my parents worry about me. It was the only thing that bothered me a lot, that my parents worry about me. And there's no way to convey a message. No way."

Once Murray learned that his parents had been killed, he used self-talk and his inner strengths to counteract his feelings of despair and to reclaim his heritage. He said, "For a while after I got out of prison camp, I was mad at God and very mad at my parents. 'Why did you take me to that place? Why did you leave me all by myself?' Especially when I had no money, when I was in the streets, begging for food, until somebody put me in an orphanage house. And I became.... For example, Jewish people are not supposed to eat certain stuff, and I said, 'Heck with it!' and I didn't pay attention to it. And then I thought to myself, 'No. I'm going to change. I want to be the way my parents raised me, not the way Hitler wanted me to be.' So I changed again, because I didn't want to be the way Hitler wanted, to completely eliminate Judaism. And I said, 'No. I'm just going to be this way. I'm going to be the way my parents taught me.'"

Circular Support: The Intersection of Inter- and Intrapersonal Support

Interpersonal support, whether instrumental or emotional, is totally focused on the other person: meeting a need, caring for, easing a burden, supplying a skill or service the other person doesn't have or have access to. Being able to set aside your own problems to reach out to others, to offer that support, requires that the giver has recognized his or her own strengths, has a positive attitude, and recognizes that he or she has something of value to give. Circular support, on the other hand, is a hybrid, a kind of the bridge between inter- and intrapersonal support. It differs from instrumental and emotional support in a critical way. Those two categories of support are voluntary actions of reaching out to others. Circular support, on the other hand, simply *happens* when, in the process of offering instrumental or emotional support, the giver discovers that he or she feels a deep satisfaction at having done something for someone else. In other words, circular support is unintended intrapersonal support. I have included three stories of circular support here to familiarize you with the concept; you will find more circular-support stories about surprising moments of kindness extended to our survivors, in Chapter Six.

Will's first POW camp was Stalag Luft III, the camp for U.S. and British officers. All sorts of information circulated among the prisoners, including an interesting piece of gossip about pilots being treated somewhat better than enlisted men, because Nazi General, Hermann Goëring, had a special interest in men of any nationality who were pilots. Conditions were still severe, but much less so than in other camps and fellow prisoners were able to offer each other emotional support. *Will* somehow obtained a small radio that could pick up BBC broadcasts late at night. Those disembodied voices speaking English were an additional source of interpersonal support—a comforting contact for the prisoners, confirming that the United States and her Allies were still alive and well and fighting for them. That news gave special urgency to the orders given to all American airmen to try and get back to friendly territory.

Will and his fellow American prisoners had many hours of unoccupied time, often filled with long discussions, debates and even some outright arguments. Since unresolved interpersonal tensions would only have added to the huge stresses the men already experienced, they collectively decided they needed someone who could settle disputes. *Will* was selected as the company arbiter and was called on whenever disagreements flared in the close quarters of prison-camp barracks. When *Will* asked why he was the person selected, his fellow prisoners said it was an obvious choice for them since he was the only one with any law-school experience. In the end, the men made a smart choice. *Will* said, "This sounds like I'm bragging, but whenever we had a dispute and it just couldn't seem to be resolved, they referred it to me." He knew that his decisions wouldn't always be popular ones, but said, "I never had one that they didn't agree on, it would be better to do that, than to do something else." His skills ended up being immensely helpful, and the work made him feel good as he saw that his actions had a positive impact.

Before World War II, Charles Mott had such extensive flying experience with the Navy that he was honored with an invitation to fly with the Flying Tigers, a highly respected group of Chinese pilots. He was captured by the Japanese army after his plane was shot down over rural China in January 1942. After parachuting out of his damaged plane, he sustained heavy injuries when he landed. He said, "I had a broken foot, broken pelvis, and broken arm. When I hit the ground, my bones broke and stuck in the ground." The Japanese confined him in a military hospital, where their philosophy was to get guys out of there as quickly as possible. They offered no extra food, no extra anything, but did treat his bouts of dengue fever and malaria. They also never set his bones, but Charles told me, "They didn't interfere with me setting it myself. I had a splint and got hold of some gauze. No traction for my foot or my arm." His bones knit back together, though one arm is now an inch shorter than the other, and he lost all movement in his foot along with his sense of balance. It took him about three months to be able to stand up.

Once Charles was mobile, he was "bunked in" with some British prisoners. All told, the work camp, named Nong Pladuk, held about 200 officers and 2,000 men, mostly all British. Their job was working on the railroads. Because Charles couldn't walk very far, he was put in charge of two Jap vehicles that the prisoners used and maintained. In the process, his experiences with the Flying Tigers came into play. He was already aware of some of the Oriental customs, courtesies, do's and don't's. He said, "I very early resolved that rather than being obdurate and sort of an unreasonable guy, I would make it a point to learn Japanese and comply with their etiquette, which includes a bow occasionally. It's a situation where they are the masters, they got the guns, and you might as well acknowledge it." In turn, the Japanese acknowledged Charles's efforts and treated him "like a guy of intelligence."

Charles's instances of circular support are unique among my interviewees. He told me that in spite of his efforts treat his Japanese captors with civility, they still beat him up. He remembered getting "bashed" twice, describing the experience in a way that clearly illustrates how circular support works. As the ranking officer of his unit in the POW camp, Charles was proud of being able to physically demonstrate his loyalty to his men by volunteering to take a beating in the place of one of his men. He told me, "There's another important thing that I discovered. I didn't realize it was there all the time; I just didn't recognize it. When you took the part of one of your troops against the Japanese and you wound up getting beat up, that's a big morale booster. You're the leader, they're loyal to you, and they understand that you are fighting the good fight for them. Loyalty breeds loyalty."

Unlike the eight brothers you met in Chapter Two, the relationship between Judith Altmann and her niece crossed generations. That added difference in years did nothing to lessen the impact of their mutual emotional support and Judith also made a conscious effort to maintain a positive attitude for the benefit of the younger girl. Doing so helped keep her own discouragement and despair at bay, a clear example of circular support. "I was with my niece all along, so we did talk whenever we had a chance. Well, had I had a choice, it would have been my father probably, but it was very special to be there with my niece, and to have her with me."

Harry and the other men in his barracks were able to offer some much-needed interpersonal support to two other men who were the object of the racial discrimination commonplace in the 1940s, even in the military. *Harry* told me, "At Zogar, Stalag Luft III, a senior officer came by one night because he knew we had two empty bunks. He said, 'This is a little different problem. I have two black American officers who need a place to stay.' There were some voices of dissent, but one of our barracks leaders said, 'You will bring them here right now.'" The two new men blended into the existing barracks unit and strong bonds were formed. *Harry* told me, "That's how I came to know this schoolteacher from New Jersey and another one from Texas, who worked for the Ag department at the University of Texas." I have been friends with both of them ever since." The circular support that grew out of this chance meeting has translated into a lifelong friendship between *Harry* and the teachers.

Notes

14. *Taipei Times,* December 13, 2003. Full-page feature article by Gavin Phipps, staff re *Steve.*
15. Braiker, Psychology Today, December 1989, p. 23
16. Ibid
17. Ibid

18. The Alfred Tibor Collection, Artist's Statement. To see the Alfred Tibor sculpture collection, visit www.alfredtibor.net.

Chapter Four

THE ROLE OF RELIGION:
WAS GOD WITH US THERE?

My spiritual journey has had some detours—yours, too, perhaps—but I always felt grounded. I was raised Baptist, the family
religion, and considered myself a believer. I even had a little
private chapel in the woods across from my house in Mansfield,
Ohio. When I was in fifth grade, I wore a path into the pine
woods, stopping there on my way home from school every day. I
would drop my book bag under a small deciduous tree trying to
flourish in the shade of the tall pines, and then follow my path to
a natural semicircle of trees where I could sit and pray or medi-
tate.

My first detour was in junior high, when I formed a special
bond with my piano teacher who was a Christian Scientist. My
mother was uneasy but still supportive, and even took me to a
Sunday service in the local Christian Science church. I was quite
taken by the writings of Mary Baker Eddy. I had anxiety issues as
a child, and found Eddy's writings so soothing that they became
my nightly reading just before bedtime.

The detours continued. By the time I got to high school, I
had become a religious generalist, a phase that was followed
shortly by the predictable religious drop-out years of many college students. Over the next thirty-two years, I became a regular
churchgoer, first in a United Church of Christ congregation, then
an American Baptist church that is now dually affiliated with
ABC/UCC. This church celebrates flexibility and inclusiveness,
allowing each worshipper to work on and refine his or her own
core beliefs. The most important one for me is this: regardless
of one's particular beliefs, it is abundantly clear to me that what
really works for us as a civilization is to live together—and, more
importantly, to worship together—with an attitude of mutual
respect and caring, as taught by so many religions. Those values
nurture both the receiver and the giver. Circular support, to be
sure.

The Range of Religious Beliefs

Early religious beliefs in a god-like presence may have developed as a way for primitive peoples to explain damaging floods or other natural disasters. The persistence of these beliefs—massaged, reworked, reflected upon, puzzled over, formalized, embodied, adapted, transformed, fought over and celebrated through the centuries—speaks to their value in easing our minds when random, negative events may disrupt familiar patterns of living and shake our sense of security. In today's world, we have access to a much wider variety of problem-solving methods than were available to our survivors. Even so, many of us still rely on our religious beliefs as well as our fellow believers for comfort in times of stress. Even though religion is personal, memorable tragic events which stop our collective heart, the ones so significant that everyone remembers exactly where they were when "it" happened, are often marked with special religious services that respond to our deep need to be together in times of crisis.

Some people believe. Some people don't. It's that simple. Whether or not you believe in God, you can scarcely help being aware of the seemingly endless varieties of religious beliefs. We believe whatever we believe based on the geographic accident of our birth, the traditions of our upbringing, the influences of our peers and our education. It is certainly possible to deal with these differing beliefs peacefully; there are 14 denominations and 16 churches in my village of 3,800 people. But religion has a dark side, too. In his book, The Demonic Turn: The Power of Religion to Inspire or Restrain Violence, author Lloyd Steffen describes the ways in which cruelty erupts among people of differing political or religious groups (Steffen, 2003). It is a pattern that goes back to the beginning of recorded history: when very strong beliefs are held regarding a particular religious faith, there has been, and continues to be, a risk that those who subscribe to that faith may become less tolerant of others who see religious matters in a different light. When such beliefs are politicized for personal, institutional or national gain, it can lead to a discounting of others' beliefs, even to the point of executing those who disagree—witness the Crusades, the Spanish Inquisition, the Holocaust and much of the contemporary Middle East, for example.

For our survivors, finding ways to connect with their faith in the midst of life on the dark side was difficult, to say the least. How was God perceived by them? Many were supported by an unshakable faith. Some had faith but wrestled with doubt. Others had no religious affiliation. In short, they held a wide variety of beliefs regarding religion, faith, God and prayer. Regardless of the degree to which they were able to rely on their religion for support, all the survivors were quite limited in their access to the kind of interpersonal support described in Chapter Two. Most of their religious activity or reflection was solitary. During the day, the silent repeating of memorized prayers, verses and sentences or very cautious, quiet talking between people were ways in which a prisoner's religious beliefs could be put to work. At night, after the guards had left the barracks, there were opportunities for communal worship. Quiet discussion of religious topics was interspersed with night singing, the familiar words of beloved old melodies comforting the singers, just as they had for centuries.

Faith and Prayer

Survivors who held deep religious convictions drew strength from their beliefs, which provided invaluable encouragement, support and comfort during difficult experiences. Their prayers to God were a way of reaching out of themselves into an area of something eternal, beyond life, beyond their little speck of risky mortal time. For *Bill*, prayers provided some badly needed comfort. He said, "We'd always pray. Even though the Vietnamese weren't really religious, we could pray, especially if we were with somebody. We would pray together or talk about when we did go to church and how highly we believed." Chuck Brutza carried a small Bible with him all during the war. He told me, "I had a small Bible in my pocket in my uniform, through all that time, in my pocket through all of these things that were happening. On the back, there's a spot about that big [gesture], it's a patch of my blood that went right through the uniform pocket."

In spite of the horrendous conditions in concentration camps, small groups of Jews used the cover of night to maintain some precious religious practices. Joe Diamond was comforted and supported by thoughts of his family and a unique combination of prayer and the Torah. He said, "What kept me going many times when I was desperate was my family. I remembered I used to be mean to my mom, and I always was praying I'd have a chance to make up once I'm free." As a Jew, Joe had a good background of scripture, especially the Pentateuch (the five books of Moses that comprise the first five books of the Christian Bible). He described it for me: "We thought about some of the stories of our people, you know, how they suffered. When I had nothing to do, I always thought about how *we* were in the desert and *we* suffered and *we* hoped. So this kept my mind busy. We stay alive and think about the miracles that God did." *Ann's* faith was strong, too: "With God's help. Everything was with God's help. I always feel… I might not practice, but I always feel it's somebody up there who helps and controls things. People say about the Holocaust, 'Where was God when this happened?' I said, 'God didn't kill people. People killed people.'"

Corwin Morey was born in 1918 and joined the Marines at a young age. He was only 22 years old when he was captured by the Japanese in the Phillipines. When I interviewed him in 2004, he was the oldest U.S. Marine veteran in Columbus, Ohio. The lasting friendships he made in the Marine Corps endured through combat, during which he earned a Purple Heart. He credits those friendships with helping him survive the Bataan Death March and then "hang on through his years in POW camps in Bataan and Corregidor." In fact, he told me he was still in close contact with his fellow Marine veterans. Corwin emphasized the particular value of prayer for him: "I wasn't very religious as far as going to church and stuff like that, before, but I always had belief in God, you know? I would say my silent prayers and stuff, and it helped. No doubt about it. You know you're going to get direction. You need the help of somebody 'higher up.'" Alfred Tibor's prayers had a singular focus: "You pray to God, 'Give me some food.' Let Him give you food before they kill you." And Michael Stroff's angel never left him: "I'm a Catholic. The Archangel Michael was my co-pilot. I prayed constantly. I depended on prayer and never had days when I couldn't cope."

Ben Lohman was born in 1918 and was in his early twenties when he was taken prisoner in the Pacific. All the Marines who were captured felt completely unprepared for being a prisoner of war, especially under the Japanese and their culture of Bushido, but Ben and five buddies stuck it out together. At every POW camp where he was held, Ben tried to take his mind off the physical and psychological abuse by watching the beautiful sunsets, lying out after dark to identify constellations like the Southern Cross, and thinking about his mother and father.

He told me his faith was by far the most help to him during this time. Ben is Catholic and he showed the St. Christopher's medal he had carried all through the war, including during his time as a POW. There were two holes worn through the medal from Ben having rubbed it so often. Being able to hold that medal in his hand was, and still is, a special reminder to him of the meaning of his faith. "I had this good background and I had a miraculous medal around my neck that ended up with two holes worn through it. Even though I had faith that I would survive, I was ready. I'd said my final prayers to St. Jude, the patron saint of hopeless cases."

God's Mysterious Messages

Murray Ebner was only twelve years old when he was sent to a concentration camp. Since he was suddenly and totally separated from his family, he thought about them a lot. He also thought a lot about God: "God was with me. God thought, 'He's too young to die.' God protected me all the time." Murray's strong faith led to a religious experience that defied explanation. It came about after three people had escaped one day. Everyone knew that meant that three other people would be hanged. But all day long, nothing happened. By nighttime, everyone was tense. Murray then painted this word picture for me: "At night, when I went to sleep, something very unusual happened to me. Something told me, something practically pushed me away from my bunk to go someplace else and sleep under a bunk. That was the most.... I mean, it would have to be from God, or my parents, or something that said, 'Don't sleep.' It was the most powerful thing. In three years, it was the only time something like this... it was forced on me. Physical jumping in my chest and I was, I was almost taken over. 'Don't sleep. Go over there.' Very intense. Unbelievable.

There was something that had to be God's hand, because my parents were not there. But it felt like my parents were talking to me. It felt as if God pushed me. Something heavy laid on my heart. Something heavy laid on my heart and it never happened before. It never happened since then."

Ann also had an inexplicable experience. Having her sister with her was invaluable, especially after everyone else in their family had been killed. The two girls looked out for each other, with *Ann* taking on the role of mother. She told me about the day the Nazis almost took her sister. On a regular basis, all the prisoners had to stand for an Appel, where the Nazis inspected everyone and selected those who would be sent to the gas chamber that day. *Ann* said, "The doctors checking each girl. If you have some blemishes, you have a scratch, if you have a birthmark or anything, they taking you out, and we know she's going to the gas chamber."

On this particular day, all the girls were instructed to take off their dresses. *Ann* told me her group did not have the blue-and-white striped coat and pants: "We just had the dress they gave us, and that's the way for weeks and weeks and weeks we were wearing the same dress." As the girls lined up, *Ann* noticed that her sister had just developed a little pimple right under her nose. It was full of pus already and very noticeable. *Ann* immediately began to worry: "How can I save mine sister? If I'm gonna touch the pimple then I will have pus and maybe blood, and she, too, and we both gonna go. I told you before, I never gave up hope. And the sky is blue, the sun is very white, almost beautiful, and we standing. And I opened my hand and in my heart I say, 'How can I save mine sister?'" Even as she said this little prayer, *Ann* looked up and saw a small square of cloth floating down towards her and her sister. She told me, "It was so white, unbelievable, and floating like. And I grabbed that piece of cloth. If this is not a miracle, what is? So I look. The doctor was a little away and I took off that pus stuff, and I throw away the cloth. And that's the way I saved mine sister from the gas chamber."

Faith

Alex Ehrmann learned that interpersonal support and religious faith can be powerful allies. He told me, "My encouragement was that I believed very deeply in God, that God is with me. And I was religious. I prayed. I prayed every day, every morning when I was marching out to work. I prayed during the work whenever I had the opportunity to be just by myself, within myself, I prayed. On the way home, I prayed. My brother mirrored back to me my own beliefs. One of the main supports, spiritual supports, for me was the fact that I saw others who had similar beliefs as I do." Alex was convinced that he would be alive when the war ended, and told me, "I was dreaming of that, and I didn't give up hope even in the darkest hour. Faith is so important that without it nothing would have meaning. If I were to rely only on my ego and my power, my capability, then I would not have any support from you but acknowledging the correctness of my view. I'd be nothing."

Marian Haszlakiewicz is unique among our Holocaust survivors: a devout Catholic held in a Nazi concentration camp. He said, "I considered that my faith absolutely helped me to go through all those ordeals. I prayed every day, and I considered that most of miracles, thanks to God's decision, because through these two years, there were so many critical moments, that it is nothing but I considered it's a miracle that I survived those things. And I strongly believe that my dedication to our faith, it was extremely helpful." (When Marian apologized to me for his somewhat insecure use of English grammar, I told him the feeling that his survival was almost miraculous had come through loud and clear.)

In the concentration camp, Marian became close friends with a Catholic priest, who was also a prisoner. The Nazis decided to send the priest to another camp, where conditions were so bad and the work was so demanding that prisoners seldom survived more than three days. Marian told me, "So, there's my friend. The Nazi commandant in charge says, 'No, he's good for nothing. He has to go. I don't need him.' So I tell him, 'Well, if you send him then I go with him, because he is my friend. I cannot let him go alone.' And he said, 'Go. You are stupid. Just go.' So I went with this guy, simply from good friendship. I didn't want to let him go alone and see for the worst there. And this is exactly where the dear God makes the decision: it turned out for him and for me, good."

Dick Mann and *Hank* both relied on their faith. Dick told me, "I'm a Christian, not all that strong, but I've always gone to church, and I really felt for those who were not. They couldn't have anyone to talk to, and I had Jesus to talk to, and that was very helpful, very helpful and meaningful to me." After *Hank* bailed out of his crippled bomber, all he could think of was his wife and family as he drifted toward the ground. He said, "If it weren't for the fact that I was pretty busy, I'd have been one sorry mess from a mental viewpoint. I remember the exact words of the prayer I kept repeating all the way down: 'God, please have mercy on me. I want to see my wife again.' The closer to the ground I got, the calmer I became. I somehow knew that He heard those words."

Charles Mott told me his religious faith as a Baptist had been an important part of his life as a child, and remained so as an adult. In the Japanese military hospital, he was given a bed on the floor in a little room. One morning, a Japanese soldier, who was also a patient, stopped at the window to Charles' room and looked around. The next day, he showed up again, carrying an English-language Bible. The soldier told Charles his name was Yasimasa Takinanga, and that he was a Christian from an area near Tokyo. As the two men talked, a surprising friendship began to emerge. Yasismasa visited frequently, often bringing Charles some toilet articles, including a toothbrush.

He shared that he was a machine gunner in the Japanese Army, attacking Burma. Charles told me, "In our conversations, it turned out that he was in fact a Christian. They had a little church in Japan and they had a sister church in the United States. So the two churches exchanged Christmas gifts, and he remembered this particular exchange: when he was a kid, he received a doll from one of the Christian kids in the United States. I was sort of their opposite number in this country. I am a Baptist and we still have sister churches in other countries. When Yasimasa was cured of whatever he had, malaria maybe, he came by in full dress with his rifle and everything and wished me good-bye."

Bob Phillips, who served as a chaplain during World War II, is now a priest. He understood that, like so many other things, liberty is not appreciated until it is taken away. Bob and his fellow soldiers were taken prisoner by the Japanese Army in the Philippine Islands and had no assurance they would survive. In fact, they later learned that their execution orders had already been signed and the date for execution had been set. He clearly remembered the day when he knew he would make it through the experience of being a POW: "The word 'grace' jumped out from the page. I felt one of those sudden reprocessing feelings— the Gestalt had shifted. Now I saw things in a new way. Grace. Gracefully. If we can do that, feel that, be that, our journey will be doable."

Religion in a Crisis

Crisis situations can be powerful motivators and dire circumstances can transform casual connections to religion into more meaningful ones. For Albert Allen, once everything else was taken away, religious faith assumed a vital role. He said, "We thought about religion a lot more. That's all you had to turn to. I mean, when you're in prison camp and you realize it, that Dad's not going to do any good, your brother or your friends or anybody. Now, I know I was very fortunate. The Lord was looking over my shoulder, helping me on that deal. There's no question, that's all I can say. It goes back to my big deal when I tell people, 'There's no atheists in foxholes.'"

When Judith Altmann first arrived at Auschwitz, she was overwhelmed with feelings of horror and shock, as her parents were quickly sent off to the gas chamber. At seventeen, she was young enough that relying on her religious faith was not her first

thought. Later on, however, she was able to have more supportive thoughts about religion: "Just hold onto faith. God will help."
Steve has some interesting views on prayer and faith: "Everything
they did to you to belittle you.... The one thing they didn't like to
see you do was praying. Oh, man, you could get hit in the back of
the head with a butt of a rifle or anything, if they seen you praying. So the only thing way you could do was just pray to yourself.
If you never prayed, you prayed there. That's the only one or the
only thing you've got. You haven't got nothing else."

When *Steve* and I talked about religion and faith, he told me
that lots of POWs wonder about why they went through that,
why they're alive and able to tell others about their experience.
Steve had a unique answer: "Well, maybe there's a greater force
than .... Maybe the way out, in plain English, like we say it,
maybe the old boy upstairs has got something else planned for us,
and just took our number and moved it way back on the pages.
But you just wonder, there's got to be something somewhere that's
pretty strong, that carries you on through, or you just wouldn't be
here."

Dealing With Doubt

Some survivors had more doubt, more skepticism about religion
than others. *Will* was one of a number of survivors who never
quite connected with religion. He said, "They went to all the services that they had which they read all their religious books, and
we had the pistol-packing padre who was a Scotsman and everybody went to that. Gee, I guess I don't get much out of sermons,
and I guess I marched to my own drummer. So I never went to
church because church was always full."

Even though her faith was still forming, Judith Altmann was
moved to be supportive when another girl asked her to pray during the chaos of an air raid. The girls were being held in a camp
in Essen, Germany, and Allied bombers were active in the area.
About 1,400 prisoners were able to go into a bunker, but only
because they were working people and the Nazis needed them.
Coincidentally, a new transport of non-Jewish women had just

come in that day. They were the last ones to get into the bunker and, therefore, the ones closest to the exit while the bombs were falling. A rabbi's daughter came to over where Judith was standing inside the bunker and asked Judith to pray with her. Judith's niece tried to discourage her from the praying: "Oh, leave her alone. What do you want? We are going to die, hopefully we'll die anyway. We want to die, because we cannot endure the hardship any longer." Judy went with the rabbi's daughter anyway, and told me: "We go into the corner, she and I, and we pray to the angel of miracles, or whatever his name is. And we pray and we pray. The bomb did come down, but did not hit one of our girls. Of course, she interpreted that it was the miracle of the prayer, yet it hit the beginning at the entrance and a lot of the newcomers were killed. So she interpreted as miracle. Of course it could be coincidence."

In the chaos of the war, Joe Diamond's faith was overtaken by doubt. He said, "I felt that God had let us down. I almost thought that a believer…. Where is this great God that we…?" In the end, it took Joe a long time to come back to religion. In fact, he was close to being an atheist for a while, and told me, "You see all these people are getting the…. We're the chosen people according to the Bible. God chose us, gave us the commandment, said, 'Here!' And they were being killed, okay? So it's a tough one, to go back to religion again." By the time I interviewed him, Joe was on a more firm religious footing. He calls himself a believer, but says he is "not exactly religious. Today, I do believe in God. There has to be a God. Change your weather, and all that. Well, it's like you have to do things on your own and God will be behind you, they claim. That's another subject altogether, like when Elie Wiesel, said, 'It was like God was on vacation.' And it took him a long time to come back, too. But we're in believers' families. We have to believe something."

Henry Greenbaum came to believe that faith and questions sometimes have to coexist: "My faith got stronger, I believe in God, but then I questioned Him, you know? 'Why did it take you so long?'" Ahmed Kathrada described himself as not particularly religious, but remembers a very meaningful sentence that was spoken during a church service on Robben Island: "I felt very sad that I had no shoes until I met a man who had no feet." For Kathrada, this familiar anonymous statement was a sudden shock for him. He had always expected that religious people would speak of God and religion in more formal ways. The words had a powerful impact though, and their meaning remained vivid to him throughout the years of his incarceration. "I never was an actively religious person. I still am not, but my belief is there. And we took solace, we took comfort from all the religions. Mr. Mandela, when we were on Robben Island, encouraged us to go to all services—Anglican, Methodist, Dutch Reform, Muslim, Hindu— out of respect for the religion itself, out of respect for the clergy persons that came. In bad weather, choppy seas, they'd come. And we did derive comfort, because they brought encouragement."

Thaddeus Stabholz gives us a vivid portrait of how his faith in God was compromised by the horror of the Holocaust. He said, "Well, I tell you what, after being about eighteen months in Auschwitz, over a million Jews killed in gas chambers. At that time I saw with mine own eyes. Every day was a transport, and I saw men, women, kids. Of course it was.... I tried to believe, but my belief got a little shaky. I thought, 'So many people going to die. Young kids.' Sometimes I want to ask, 'My God, where are you?' A slaughter you cannot imagine. Four crematoria, two hundred yards from the camp, and you can see day and night smoke belching into the air, the terrific stench of burning bodies. I had to smell it day and night. Also the smoke covering the camp, day and night, day and night, for eighteen months.

"Because you thought, in 1944, that all Jews in Europe were going to be killed. So instead of things getting improved, you saw everything getting worse. And I don't know if you could accept it, but after so long a time, you see 10,000 killed every single day, so after a while you just...ah.... But the more you see, your heart, your brain, your soul, you see the injustice. You feel so bad. You are completely helpless. You cannot do a thing. You pray for something. Nothing happened. The more we prayed, the more people died, so it was just a letdown. So you think you are not good enough to pray because your prayers are not answered. I was never a devout Jew, but still, when I pray, not only for myself but for those hundreds of thousands of people, especially kids. But you know, it didn't help much."

Jacob Hennenberg, whose thoughts about the nature of memory opened the Introduction, was born in 1924 in the Polish city of Oswiecim, now called Auschwitz. He was fifteen years old in 1939 when the Nazis invaded Poland, and seventeen in March 1941 when they relocated all the Jews who lived in Auschwitz to the ghetto in Chrzanow, in occupied Poland. Jacob stayed there only two months before being relocated to a labor camp in Wiesau, Germany, in May 1941—the last time he ever saw his father or three of his four sisters. He also was in three other work camps besides Wiesau, including Klettendorf, where he shoveled snow off the Autobahn.

At Waldenburg, concentration camp #64, Jacob learned that all the prisoners would be getting an ID number. He remembers that everyone was told, "From now on you are only numbers. No name. No country." Since Jacob's Jewish faith was very important in his life, he searched his mind for a way to make that anonymous number have some meaning. He decided to pin his hopes on getting the number eighteen because, in Hebrew, letters are also numbers. The letters that comprise the number eighteen, "Het" and "Jud," spell "Chai" which means life. The number he received was not eighteen, but 64242…which adds up to eighteen.

Years after the war, Jacob wrote a long prayer in which he worked out his feelings about the Creator. I have included it here in its entirety.

"Creator of the universe, over fifty years ago I was liberated from my bondage…. I do not forgive the killers and their accomplices, but I no longer look at every passerby with suspicion any more. How about my faith? What hurt me was your absence and your silence. Thinking while in the camps about the words ELI ELI LAMA AZABTANU[19] that my grandfather, Henoch Hennenberg, constantly played on his gramophone before the war. In my childhood, I did not expect much from

human beings. But I expected everything from you. What was going on in the heavens while your children were marked for humiliation only because they were Jewish? These questions were still haunting me. You have many defenders with all kinds of explanations and reasons. I reject them all. Auschwitz will forever be a question mark only. It cannot be comprehended with or without G-D. At one point, I began wondering. Auschwitz was not something that came down from the heavens. It was conceived by men, implemented by men, staffed by men. And their aim was not only to destroy us, but you as well. Ought we not think of your pain, watching your children suffer at the hands of your other children?"[20]

Notes

19. To see the Alfred Tibor sculpture collection, visit www.alfredtibor.net.

20. Excerpt from *Tell Us, Papa, What Happened There,* undated self-published memoir by Hennenberg.

Chapter Five

UNEXPECTED OVERTURES:
SURPRISING MOMENTS OF KINDNESS

The process of research is fascinating. It is always satisfying to find the exact information I need, but I love it when my research surprises me. During the interviews, I had two such surprises. The first was hearing stories of unexpected kindnesses offered to a survivor by an enemy combatant or a prison-camp guard or a civilian who was either a co-worker in one of the German factories or lived near a camp. You will read about the second surprise in the next chapter.

Through the previous chapters, you and I have taken a close-up look deep within the chaos of human conflict. After the descriptions of once-unimaginable cruelty inflicted both on military personnel and innocent civilians, the stories in this chapter give me hope. I was truly touched the first time one of the participants told me about someone initiating a peaceful interaction, and my wonder increased with each successive story. Even though I did almost all the interviews for this book and know all the stories, I find myself coming back to this chapter again and again. Just as Stanley Milgram discovered that we can be cruel, I am reassured that there also is a basic goodness in us all, even though it may take the most extreme of circumstances to bring it out. The extending of kindness often happened to just one survivor, but I would like to start by sharing two stories about entire nations offering kindness to large groups of people.

The KinderTransport

This story of the KinderTransport was written by Emmy and Harry Loeb, who shared it with me. Both Harry and Emmy survived Nazi Germany because of this initiative that rescued 10,000 Jewish children and sent them to England. Heinz Adolf "Harry" Loeb was born to Emil and Matilda Loeb on February 19, 1922 in Ehringshausen, Germany. His sister, Erna, was eight years old when her brother was born. Erna had registered for immigration to the United States in 1935, and Harry's parents did the same in 1936. Harry attended a Jewish vocational school in Frankfurt am Main until the infamous Kristallnacht, on November 9, 1938, changed everything. At the age of sixteen, Harry saw his dorm at the school go up in flames, along with virtually all Jewish businesses, schools and homes. He moved in with his sister while his parents considered their options to protect Harry from the looming war. They made the wrenching decision to send Harry out of the country with the KinderTransport and kissed him goodbye on May 1, 1939, not knowing if they would ever see their son again. Erna's immigration papers came through before her parents' did and she left Germany in November 1939; Emil and Matilda followed in October 1941.

Harry eventually made it to the U.S. but his path was hardly a straight line. In June 1940, the British government interned him as an "enemy alien." He was released in January 1941 and went to work in an aircraft factory in Liverpool, a classified job which prevented him from leaving England. Then, in the fall of 1945, Harry volunteered to serve with the U.S. Military Government in Germany. After 18 months in that post he was finally able to leave and join his family in New York. By 1950, Harry had met Emmy Sigall, another KinderTransport survivor. The two were married in 1950 after having lived their separate lives on parallel tracks for over two decades.

Harry and Emmy begin their story of the KinderTransport with a brief history of the events that led to its inception. Hitler came to power in Germany in 1933. Within a short time, he had invalidated the German constitution and enacted the Nuremburg Laws, isolating the German Jewish community by classifying them as a fictitious "Non-Aryan" race and prohibiting all interaction between Aryans and non-Aryans. Most Jewish children were expelled from public schools in 1936 (the same year I started first grade). Jewish efforts to emigrate to other countries were thwarted by the worldwide depression and, in some countries, by blatant anti-Semitism. In November 1938, Kristallnacht, the "night of broken glass," saw the wholesale destruction of everything Jewish in "every corner of the Reich (Gilbert, 2006)". Synagogues were set on fire, Jewish institutions and schools were destroyed, homes and business were smashed and looted.

Emigration became imperative, especially for the endangered children, widely regarded as the most precious resource of the Jewish people. The Central Committee for German Jews[21] had already begun to appeal to foreign governments to take in an unspecified number of Jewish children as refugees. One country after another turned them down but, finally, England said yes. The British Parliament passed a "bill" granting temporary asylum for up to 10,000 Jewish children from Germany. To guard against dependence on British governmental financial support, each child's sponsor had to post a monetary guarantee from non-German sources. Even though the Nazi government granted permission for the program and issued proper travel documents for the children, ages six months to seventeen years, to leave the country, they insisted that information about KinderTransport could not be publicized in any form. In short, the transports were to be conducted discreetly and without knowledge of the general public. Families were normally informed by word of mouth, with very short notice, when the departure of a transport was announced. Obviously, children living in larger cities had a distinct advantage over those in rural areas, especially as telephone communications were no longer allowed.

This is truly a "which cliff?" dilemma, as described by Emmy and Harry: "To those parents who were unable to emigrate in a given time frame, the opportunity to send a child to relative safety must have been desired by many. Others could not bear to be separated at such critical stages of their children's lives. And there was also the realization that a parent might never see their child again. All of these factors led to very painful, heartbreaking decisions. Harry and Emmy described it this way: "Those decisions, made by adults for the good of their children, had overwhelming unintended consequences for the children. While the parents were left in Germany to deal with their own strong emotions and the cruelties of Nazism, the children were utterly unprepared to cope with what was happening to them. The parting was almost always highly emotional for parent and child. Children were allowed to take a small suitcase and the equivalent of $2.50 in German currency. Jewelry and any sort of precious metals were not permitted. It was utterly confusing to the younger children, and some felt abandoned by their elders. Many of the school-age children felt devastated. A few of the older ones thought of it as an adventure."

The first transport, an entire Jewish orphanage, left Berlin in December 1938, only four weeks after Britain had formally agreed to provide asylum. The Loebs' narrative continues: "The children were placed into special railroad coaches attached to regularly scheduled trains for travel to Holland. Usually, there was no adult supervision on the trains. The older children were told to look after younger ones. Once over the Dutch border, nurses and other aid personnel came aboard. The train ride ended at the ferry terminal at Hook-of-Holland where an overnight ferry took the children to Harwich on the English east coast. From there another train was taken to London. At this point, a newly created Jewish Aid agency took responsibility." The youngest children were placed in foster homes. School-age children were sent to boarding schools, if they were lucky, or to orphanages and private homes. The older children were accommodated in youth hostels, on farms and in agricultural camps. The Society of Quakers (Friends) played a significant role in the placement of the children, providing numerous homes.

Transports varied in size and frequency but they came to a sudden halt with England's declaration of war against Germany on September 3, 1939. The last transport arrived on September 2. In all, over 9,000 children had been saved but that did not mean that all was suddenly well for them. As Harry and Emmy said, "After the arrival in Britain, many of the children encountered emotional problems. They were unable to communicate due to language difficulties. Cultural differences became social obstacles. Correspondence with their parents was extremely slow and cumbersome. And then the war broke out, making it even more difficult, if not impossible, to correspond with parents or relatives. In 1941-42, most parents still residing in Germany or Austria were deported to concentration camps and, thus, all contact between parent and child ceased, forever in most cases. These were truly agonizing times for many children."

The Loebs tell us that many of the older boys served in the British forces during the war. Most of the very young were adopted by their foster parents when it was ascertained that their own parents had perished. Some 2,000 left Britain for the U.S., their original intent, after the war ended. Others went to Israel shortly after its creation. Most have become productive and respected citizens of the U.K. In spite of having been among the rescued children, Harry and Emmy were determined to give voice to all the ones who weren't saved: "These successes must be measured against the complacency of the civilized world, countries which failed to provide a safe haven for the 100,000 Jewish children of Central Europe. These children could have been saved from certain annihilation prior to World War II. Unfortunately, they became part of some 1.5 million child Holocaust victims who could not be rescued after the genocide was in full swing."

The Danish Rescue

The second story is widely known as the Danish Rescue. I learned of it when I interviewed Jacob Hennenberg and he showed me the book his family had compiled and published, filled with his personal stories of the war years. One of the stories, though, isn't personal at all. In fact, he didn't hear of it until 1995, fifty years after the war, when he and a friend took a trip to Europe. On their way home, they stopped in Denmark and learned of the 1943 Danish Rescue, when an assortment of Danish private boats secretly ferried the Jews of Denmark across the five-mile strait to refuge in Sweden. As with the KinderTransport story, a little background will be helpful here.

Denmark was invaded and occupied by the German Army in the spring of 1940. Since there was little resistance by the Danish people, the Danish government was allowed to continue to function. On September 18, 1943, Hitler decided that it was time for Danish Jews to be deported to Auschwitz. The Danish people disagreed. They were united in their determination to rescue the Danish Jews, and no Danish police or armed force would cooperate with Hitler's order. In short, while appearing to carry on with business as usual, the government and the people refused to implement German anti-Jewish laws and round up the approximately 6,500 Danish Jews. SS troops had to be sent from Germany to Denmark because even the Wehrmacht commander,

General Von Hanneken, refused to obey, arguing that the task of rounding up the Jews was not a military one.

On September 28th, the Jewish New Year, advance notice of the impending SS deportation round-up was announced to Jewish congregations in all the synagogues. At the same time, the Danish government threatened armed resistance against the SS if they were to violate any Danish laws, particularly the one that prohibited forced entry into any Danish home. Two nights later, when the SS police went door to door to round up Jews, the Jews simply did not answer the door, forcing the SS to move on. Only 477 Jews were caught and sent to Auschwitz.

What happened to the rest of them is the story of the Danish Rescue. Jacob tells the story well: "On October 14, 1943, the Swedish government promised to grant sanctuary to Danish Jews. It led to one of the most remarkable rescues in history. First, doctors, teachers, businessmen, students, housewives, farmers, taxi drivers, etc., mobilized the Danish fishing fleet to take Jews across the Sund, the body of water separating Sweden from Denmark. Next, they moved Jews secretly to beaches and ports of departure. They raised money to pay for the crossing (about $100 per person); Danish police stood guard to ward off danger; taxi drivers drove Jews to the ports so as not to arouse suspicion; druggists supplied free stimulants to keep people awake all night. By the end of October, Denmark had rescued 7,220 Jews, including over 800 German Jewish refugees who had come to Denmark before 1940 and 686 non-Jewish spouses of Jews."

How Moments of Kindness Arise

Skills in my profession must be constantly updated and refined. Through the years, I read copiously and took numerous continuing education courses that kept me abreast of advances in counseling and clinical psychology. I also "went to school" in the process of every counseling session. My experience with each client was a unique blend of the expected and the unexpected. While no counseling was involved in any of the interviews that are the foundation for this book, I observed the same fascinating mix of the expected and the unexpected.

As the number of interviews piled up, so did my increasing familiarity with the generalities and specifics of the Holocaust, POW camps and the global political landscape in the 1960s and beyond. Each interview, examined through the lens of my professional life, informed my next interview. Taken as a whole, both the professional client sessions and the research interviews give me a broad frame of reference for discerning and identifying patterns of behavior. I can see the connections between efforts on the scale of the KinderTransport and the Danish Rescue and one-on-one moments of kindness. Those individual moments are clear illustrations that circumstances can create opportunities for people on opposing sides of a conflict to view a previously anonymous enemy as a person, even though battlefields, POW camps and Holocaust camps are unlikely sources of kindness.

As a POW in the Philippines, Albert Allen was part of the Bataan Death March—75 miles of forced march with no food, no water. Many of the prisoners were injured; all of them were starving. It was common knowledge that if you fell down or even just fell behind, you would be shot or bayoneted. By the time Albert finally couldn't go any further, regardless of the threat of death, the line of march had split into several sections, with a hundred yards or so between them. Albert told me, "It was terrible. I laid down in a ditch about 100 feet from two other Americans who were being sick. I was about half gone and I fell asleep. I heard this yelling, this screaming, and by god, here are two or three Japanese soldiers, bayoneted these two Americans that I had first saw. And they were really bad. They couldn't even get up. I thought, 'Well, I gotta move.'"

Gathering his strength, Albert waited for the next group of prisoners, got up and fell into line. After about a quarter of a mile, he fell out again. He said, "I went off the road pretty far and got back in these bushes and I laid down there. And the same deal, I kind of passed out. The next thing I knew, I heard this 'Cooda! Cooda!' I looked up and here was this Japanese, a rather young one, who had his rifle and his bayonet. And 'Whsst! Whsst!', and he was sticking me right here [gesture] and going pretty good there." Albert told me that this moment was the lowest point of his POW experience. Even though the bayonet never went clear through him, he said he wouldn't have cared "one bit" if it had. But then he went on to say, "I'm sure once he'd have got it in, I would have thought different, but I was ready to give up completely."

To Albert's surprise, the Japanese soldier suddenly stopped stabbing him, propped his rifle against a nearby bush, and pulled out his canteen. The expression on his face never changed, but he held out the canteen, offering it to his prisoner. Albert remembers, "I took it and knew he wanted me to take a drink. I thought it was going to be sake. A lot of the Japanese drink it, an alcohol drink. I thought, 'Oh boy, that's all I need.' Well, it turned out it was probably the worst thing I could have had. It was goat's milk. It was sour, it was terrible, but I took it. Then he took it back, and of course I thanked him, 'Aurigacho.'"

Even though Larry Bott was a medic, he often was given other duties between battles. He described one particular assignment: "I will never forget this ridge when our company ran out of water. Sgt. Dunham and another sergeant decided to arm themselves to the teeth and took me along to carry a five-gallon jerry can. We had to go through L Company out to no-man's land in a deep ravine. The path zig-zagged down about 500 feet to the bottom where there was a well. While the two sergeants kept guard, I filled the can and we walked back up the path. About halfway up, we stopped to rest. When we looked back down at the well, there were two Germans getting water from the same well as we had. We didn't fire at them, and they never noticed us. That night, when all was quiet on this same mountain, we could hear a German playing 'Lili Marlene' on his harmonica."

Through the course of his combat service in Germany, Chuck Brutza had an increasing admiration for the job done by the unarmed Army medics as they cared for the wounded in the midst of battle. At first, the Germans honored the Geneva Convention provisions about not harming anyone wearing the Red Cross insignia. When the war began to go against them, however, "they shot anything and everything that was the enemy" and killed a lot of the combat medics. Chuck's commanding officer called everyone in the 45th together and said, "I need another favor from you guys. We need 30-40 more combat medics. And we don't have time to train you beyond the basics. In other words, stop the bleeding and get the f*** out of there."

Chuck and some of his fellow riflemen who volunteered for the job were pulled out of combat, flown back to Indiana, and taught the basics of being a medic. Armed with what little knowledge they were able to acquire, they went back to the "lion's den" with the 45th Division, and went out as combat medics, knowing full well that the red-cross insignia on their uniforms and helmets had ceased to be a magic shield. Chuck was captured in the middle of a battle. He remembers, "I was patching up one of our guys when the Germans came through and I got shot. I was bleeding pretty bad, and the Germans came over and put tourniquets on my leg to stop the blood." All the prisoners taken that day were transported to a nearby town and sheltered in a building overnight. The whole time, Chuck was wondering what would happen to him, and he told me, "I was thinking the worst of the enemy. Maybe they'd blow my brains out or something, I don't know."

The next morning, some German medics arrived. After making sure Chuck had no weapons, they took him to a nearby hospital and sat him down, still in what he called his "muddy stinky uniform." There were two or three nurses standing around, who had no idea what to do with him, having never encountered "the enemy" inside their hospital. Then, a doctor came in. Chuck said, "He comes over to me and says, 'What have we got here?' He's looking at me in my filthy uniform and he's talking in German. I get a word or two, and I can see he's angry at somebody and I'm thinking, 'Geez, that's all I need, an angry enemy.'" It turned out that the doctor was angry at the nurses, not at Chuck. He called some other nurses over and yelled at all of them, then gave them all a big hug, unable to be angry at his nurses for very long.

The doctor then came over to Chuck, who told me, "He taps me on the head and he says, 'You have Mama? Papa?' I don't know what the hell to think now, but I said, 'Mama and Papa? Yeah.' 'Good, good,' he says. 'We will help you. Don't be afraid. We'll help you. I'm going to tell the nurses to clean, clean, clean.

And I'll be back tomorrow.'" The nurses sprang into action, saying, "Come, come, come, come!" Three of them took Chuck into a big shower, and he remembers, "They wore bathing suits and I went in there bare naked, you know. They washed me all down and then they cleaned me up. And next morning my uniform was spotlessly clean. They washed it and dried it, did everything else. And I put it on. I looked human again." In the morning, when the doctor came back, he was pleased with what he saw. Then he said, "You know, I got good news. Good news! The war almost finis. Kaput. Almost no more war. No more. And you go home to your mama and papa." He tapped Chuck three times, and he said, "Goodbye, my friend. Goodbye, my friend."

Carl Cossin's moment of battlefield kindness came with a literal kick in the pants from a Korean officer. The Koreans were marching their American prisoners to a POW camp. Many of the captives had bad feet, terrible cuts and swelling that meant they couldn't keep up with the line of march. One night, the march stopped near a big hole in the ground that served as straw-covered winter storage for turnips. The next day, the men with bad feet were told to sit around the turnip hole without their shoes on while they waited for an ox cart to take them to the Peoples Hospital.

The American major in Carl's section of 50 men sent Carl to help load the men onto the ox cart. When he got to the turnip hole, he sat down with the rest of the prisoners but left his shoes on. He told me, "Well, I'm settin' there with shoes on and these other guys has got their feet cracked open, reddish-blue in color, and they got their feet down in this straw." A guard came up to the turnip hole and made Carl take his shoes off. When he saw that Carl's feet were in good shape, he started cussing Carl out for trying to fake it and get out of the march. When a Korean officer joined the two men, the guard told him about Carl. Carl said, "The officer motioned for me to go with my section. When I went to bend over to grab my shoes, he kicked me in the rear end and I went out on my hands and knees. I got up and took off a-runnin' for the section. I ran up to the major and told him, 'Damn you, you're gonna get me killed.' I looked over my shoulder and heard the gun a-crackin' and saw them guys fallin' forward on their faces into that turnip hole. So you see, the Korean officer kicked me and got me outta there to keep them from shooting me 'cause I had good feet. But he shot those guys. So that was the 'Peoples Hospital.'"

Fred grew up in northeast Ohio before he enlisted in the Air Force. He was trained as a paratrooper stateside and then shipped out to combat in Europe. His unlikely and surprising encounter with some German soldiers was the beginning of a lifelong friendship. On the day of the Allied invasion of France, *Fred* and his fellow paratroopers jumped from their U.S. transport plane into the French countryside. As he floated downward, the men and equipment of the German Army were clearly visible below. Luckily, *Fred* was not hit by any of the German bullets aimed at the paratroop squad.

In spite of his best efforts to steer himself to a safe landing in the shelter of the trees, away from the German tanks below him, a sudden guest of wind landed him right on top of a German half-track—a tank-like vehicle with "caterpillar" treads on the rear wheels only. The two surprised occupants of the half-track popped open their hatch, rifles at the ready, to see what had hit them. *Fred* was waiting for them, his own rifle ready. Nobody fired. Instead, the three men shared surprised looks and a short burst of laughter. The Germans took *Fred* prisoner, delivered him to a POW camp and returned to visit him whenever they could. Their friendship grew, and after the war, *Fred* visited each of their homes in Germany and they came to see him in Ohio.

Moments of kindness were rare in the all the German prison camps, but they did happen occasionally. Murray Ebner was just twelve years old when he was transported to a concentration camp. He was just old enough to be considered a good worker and, therefore, not sent to the gas chamber. When he first came to the camp, he thought a lot about escaping. Knowing he needed to know more about the routines of the guards, he hid himself in a big pile of furniture, about 100 yards away from the fence. He told me, "I went to observe what's happening, how the guards are changing and the lights going back and forth. I hid myself in the pile of furniture, laying there and looking around, probably a half hour. And all at once, I sensed somebody was behind me, and then I turned around and there's the guard with his rifle pointing right at me. And he just said, 'Raise your hands.' And I did." The guard searched him but, of course, found nothing. Murray remembers thinking that he got out of this situation because he was only thirteen years old. He said, "I'm positive if he would have seen that person, let's say eighteen, twenty, fifty, or thirty years old, he would have shot him immediately. But he seen a kid that was only thirteen and I just came to camp. And he took me back to the barracks. He says, 'Next time you do that again, well, you're going to be dead.' So he may have had some kind of feeling he didn't want to shoot a kid."

Ann also was taken to a concentration camp as a child, loaded into a cattle car to be transferred from one camp to another. At the station, on the platform between two trains, a German soldier was observing the loading process. All the girls were crammed into a car that had a little opening on the side, but only because of a missing board. She said, "So he looked in, and he throws into me a piece of bread, but I never got it because the girls grabbed. So it shows how some humanity was there, or maybe just some teasing. But I like to think about the good side, not about the bad side. But you can do it either way. You can see it either for goodness of his heart, or purposely to tease you, because what this piece of bread meant to us with so many kids around. On the good side, always the positive side."

In the winter of 1942, when Jacob Hennenberg was being held in the Klettendorf camp, he was part of a work group that cleared snow, by hand, from the Autobahn between Breslau and Berlin. On one trip back to camp, he was sitting on the back of the truck with a guard, trying to figure out how to let his family know he was alive. He asked the guard to take his picture, in exchange for a blanket given to him by his Aunt Lola, and to send the picture to his sister. The guard agreed, and the next day Jacob gave the guard the blanket, along with his sister's address.

Approximately 50 years later, while vacationing in Florida, Jacob got a big surprise: "I was standing with a group of survivors on a sandy beach in Miami, sharing with each other episodes during World War II. A man walks out of the ocean after his swim. As he came closer, they tell me that he is from the town of Kenty. I said to him, 'I was in camp Klettendorf with a man from Kenty, by the name of Leon Ramer. As a matter of fact, we were together in the same barracks.' He looks at me and exclaims, 'I am Leon Ramer!' I show the photo taken in 1942, shoveling snow, in which he is also on the photo. The whole group stood there in amazement. One survivor said it was probably the only photo of inmates in Nazi camps, and alive to tell about it. All because of Aunt Lola's blanket."

Joe Diamond remembers a harrowing episode when Red Cross officials came to the barracks to take some information from the prisoners. They sat behind a desk, and Joe and his fellow condemned were standing in line. Joe was upset, his whole body shaking. They asked him his name and where he was from. All of a sudden, there was an unexpected tap on his shoulder. He looked back and this gentleman says to him, "I'm going to save you." Joe remembers thinking, "It was like somebody sent from God. I asked him why and the man could only reply with 'I don't know.'" Joe could think of only one explanation for this miracle. "I just feel like maybe I reminded him of his kid."

The man who saved his life was actually a civilian. He had murdered two women and the concentration camp was doubling as his prison. His work assignment was to be a guard, in charge of the Jews. Remembering the moment he was told that his group would be killed by midnight, yet he would be saved, Joe said, "Even though this guy was a killer, it seems like he had a heart, too." The man made Joe go up high in the barracks and hide. About midnight, he gave Joe a signal to jump out of a window 20 feet above the ground. Joe landed safely and crawled on his stomach until he got to a row of outhouses. Outside this structure, he saw a Russian prisoner who was in charge of the latrine. Joe said, "Could you hide me? Because if you don't, I'm going to be taken away." The man told him to get into the hole of the latrine. A fifteen-foot hole, full of human waste. Joe went down there and the man nailed the top down in case the Germans came in. Joe was sealed in with no fresh air and the bad smell, hoping to God that the next day the man would let him out. He did. Then Joe mingled with the remaining prisoners and went back to work with the group.

Charles Mott's "moment of kindness" actually became an extended peaceful interlude. During Charles's time as a prisoner, he developed the ability to relate quite comfortably with the enemy Japanese personnel in the area. Many of those men became interested in learning English. Charles somehow made it clear to the Japanese officials that he was willing to teach them some English words. In the process of doing so, he became genuine friends with some Japanese military people. Ben Lohman, who was also held in a Japanese POW camp, found himself the beneficiary of decades-old American missionary work in Japan. Over a period of many years, the missionaries had established numerous Christian churches. As luck would have it, a child from a Christian Japanese family, who became a high officer in the Japanese army during World War II, was assigned to run the POW camp where Ben was confined. During his time there, the officer made arrangements for a Japanese Catholic priest from Tokyo to come out and celebrate a Christmas Eve mass. Every prisoner attended. The Japanese officer in charge was remarkable in his ability to think beyond the details of his complicated role as the manager of hundreds of enemy captives. He used this opportunity to honor the spiritual lives of everyone present, including himself. During that Mass, both sides joined in worship of a common God. No guns were fired, no one was injured or killed, and some war-weary soldiers on both sides experienced a single hour of peace.

Bill also taught English to his guards during his long years of incarceration in North Vietnam. Once several of his guards had expressed interest in learning English, a trade was developed: *Bill* taught some English to the guards and, in exchange, they wrapped a few precious cigarettes in foil and fastened them to the top of the toilet bucket used by the prisoners before returning it to them. *Bill* said, "Sometimes, some guards give me a pack of cigarettes to split between three guys. We'd keep them hid, because you learn that you have to be greedy and really sneaky. We'd hide them in some stupid spot."

Steve told me a story about an unexpected Ohio college connection from his days as a prisoner in Schwangford, Germany. During an air raid, *Steve* was standing outside the door of the shelter with the rest of the prisoners. The muzzle of a machine gun, pointing out, was visible in the doorway. *Steve* said, "I'm there and I nudged the guy beside of me and I said, 'I'd sure like to meet one of these sons of bitches that could speak English.' And just about that time I felt this gun go right in my ribs. I looked around and he said, 'I'll talk to you.' Well, right about then I thought, 'Well, I've just about had it now! I shouldn't have called him a son of a bitch.'"

The guard asked *Steve* where he was from. Following military procedure, *Steve* responded with name, rank, and serial number. The guard tried again, asking if *Steve* was from the United States. When *Steve* said he was, the guard assured him this was not an interrogation and asked if *Steve* had ever heard of a state called "Oheeo" and the town of Bowling Green. *Steve* told me, "Well, I just about passed out, because my home town is Findlay, Ohio, only twenty-five miles from Bowling Green. So he set the gun down, and he starts talking to me. He had taken his college training in Bowling Green, Ohio. He told me more about Bowling Green and about Findlay than I really knew myself. He told me all about the oil companies and all the oil refineries around Findlay and everything. Oh, yeah, he knew everything. After the war, a lot of people ask me what was his name. I said, 'Hey, the guy didn't even give me his phone number!'" I asked *Steve* how he felt when the guard put his gun down and talked to him. His answer surprised me. "Hurt. Really hurt. How could a man come over to the United States, have everything as nice as he had it there, then turn around and be a traitor? I must say, the man was a traitor and he should be shot. How could a man do something like that, even if it was for money, you know? You just don't know."

Almost eighteen months after my interview with *Steve*, I was amazed to hear another story about an Ohio college connection from Albert Allen. After being captured, there were new stresses to be dealt with as Albert adapted to life in the POW camp, where the threat of death or torture was a daily reality. Even in that atmosphere, a brief moment of relaxation could be had by smoking a cigarette. While the POWs had no access to cigarettes, they had unlimited access to cigarette butts dropped by the Japanese soldiers. The problem was, how to hold them long enough to enjoy the smoke. Albert told me, "We'd use these little aluminum things and we'd make little cigarette holders. If you got caught, that could be a real rough one. Depends who caught you and what they were feeling like. You could be put in the brig there, with the water thrown on the floor, forty below zero. You could be beat around by the right officer. They never took their sabers out of their scabbards, but they would leave the scabbard on and they'd beat you with that. It was like a steel club."

Albert had some time to kill one day and was using a tiny piece of aluminum to make a cigarette holder. The guard who caught him at it was just about to hit him when Albert looked down at the soldier's sweater. He said, "The guy had a crest of Oberlin College in Ohio. At that time, Oberlin and Wooster, where I went, were almost equals [in Ohio] as far as battling each other for scholastic standing or who was ahead of the other, and we played basketball and everything. So, I told him my relationship there. Well, he kind of forgot about hitting me."

Another Jacob Hennenberg story actually involves three separate moments of kindness, spread over four years. It starts in January 1941, with a knock on the gate to Jacob's family home. Two German policeman stood there, one of whom, Walter Stark, was close friends with Jacob's father. The two men had come to this Jewish residence at great personal risk, defying the government's edict that every Jewish house was off-limits unless some official function was being served. Jacob took the men in to see his father: "They took off their coats and put their guns aside and said to my father, 'Things will get very bad soon for the Jewish people.' They were willing to get for me so-called Aryan papers and send me to the town that they are from, which was Waldenburg, and employ me there until the end of the war, and then send me home." Jacob's father told them he appreciated their efforts, but that Jacob was his only son and "wherever we go, we would go together." Walter Stark took a small calendar out of his pocket, inscribed with the contact information of his firm in Waldenburg, and the address, Garten Str. 6. He said to Jacob, "If you are ever in that area, my house is open for you." With that, the two policemen left.

During the war, between 1941 and 1945, Jacob was confined to a concentration camp. One day, after work, his group marched through Waldenburg on the way back to camp. From a distance, Jacob saw a small boy playing on the sidewalk. He told me, "As we were nearing to the spot where the boy was playing, I said to my friend, Arthur, 'You see this boy playing? This is Horst Maetzig, for whom I was babysitting, while still living in Auschwitz town and carrying water for the German police.' Arthur said to me, 'Do not be silly. It is now four years later. How would you know?'" The next evening, as the group marched back from work, the same boy was playing on the sidewalk. Jacob said, "Something came over me when I reached where the boy was. I exclaimed, 'Horst!', which was his name. He looked at me and ran into the house. Arthur said, 'You will get us both killed here. All the SS has to see or hear you talking to someone. They shoot people for less than that.'" Next day, Jacob again passed the same location. He continued, "Now, Horst and his mother are standing there. When we got across from them, I tipped my cap and they nodded, acknowledging and recognizing me. Until Liberation, Elizabeth Maetzig and Horst were standing there as we passed by. To me it was a tremendous boost to my morale, because at least somebody knows that I am alive."

In May 1945, Jacob was liberated from the concentration camp. He told me, "I found the place in Waldenburg, Garten Str.

6, that Walter Stark told me about. I knocked on the gate. The Germans were afraid to open the gate for fear of reprisals by the freed prisoners. I continued knocking and an old lady came to the door. Through the closed door, I told her that I knew Walter Stark and I asked her if he is back from the war. She said he was not back, but his wife is there. She came to the door. I told her who I was and she replied that she remembered me, and they opened the door and let us in. They fed us. We took a warm bath, after such a long time not taking a bath. In no time, we became civilized again."

Stanley Wiczyk's survival depended on a lie and the willing complicity of both friends and strangers. He was a young Jewish physician, unable to find work in Warsaw after the Nazi edict that no one could hire a Jew. Stanley turned to a friend, a Ukrainian physician, for help. What he got was a letter of introduction to someone in another city and assurance from the Ukrainian doctor that this other man could hire him. When Stanley looked at the letter, which had been given to him in an unsealed envelope, he understood why: the letter never mentioned that he was Jewish. In the new city, Stanley met a woman who was a Polish Catholic. She took him to her church, where he was promised safety and protection. Stanley told me, "I was surrounded by people who created this small community and defended me. There were parishioners who would come to the priest and say, 'Father, there are people talking that the doctor and his wife are Jews.' And he would say, 'People! This is a shame! Don't repeat this! I have known them from before they were older. They are good Christians. Don't you ever mention this!' Priests in a small place like this have much power. We owe those people our life. And I make sure that my grandchildren and great-grandchildren know who rescued their grandparents."

Stanley developed a close friendship with the priest. The two would talk late into the night, over a bottle or two of vodka. Then, the priest would say, "Go home, sleep well and come back in the morning, because the morning is smarter than the evening." Stanley held back certain parts of his story from the priest, though he hinted that there would come a time when he would share everything. The priest never asked, but Stanley finally felt the time was right. He told me, "Then one time, I was behind him and never saw his face, and I think to myself, 'Now is time for me to tell him.' I said, 'Father, I am a Jew.' I never saw his face because I was behind. For me, I don't know how long, this was. Hours, each minute. And then he says, in a changed voice, 'I don't give a damn. I love you.' Great time."

Food From Unlikely Sources

On a few occasions, some prisoners had the privilege of going to the nearest village by themselves. For example, *Harry* and his fellow POWs were permitted to go from their camp to the nearby town, where guards were stationed around to watch them. *Harry* told me, "Right in front of a church there was a small road through this small village. People started to go into the church, so I just went up the walk to the church door. My buddy and I went in and sat down in a rear pew on the left side. As we came back down the walk after the service ended, a man and a woman in front of us motioned to us to follow them. They took us to a house where someone had prepared a dinner. They sat us down in their dining room, between them and their two children, and served the food. I hadn't shaved in three weeks. I was in a shambles, my clothes were filthy. Just then, I saw the food was quite sparse. I thought to myself, 'They've invited me here. I'm taking food from these children. I'm taking food from these children.'"

I vividly remember the intensity of *Harry's* emotion as he told me about the children and the food. The gesture, made at great sacrifice to that German family, so impressed him that he was able to take this act of kindness from one German family and apply it to all German people. As he put it, "I'm not a hater. Some people seem to enjoy being that way but I never did hate. I personally never felt any irrational hate for German people. They were victims, as we were. To me, there were many Germans who helped people on forced marches, with pails of water or a half-loaf of bread."

Food was constantly on every prisoner's mind, regardless of the setting or the war. It is easy for us to think of concentration and

POW camps as islands, isolated from everything, but that was not always the case. Often, there were nearby cities and villages, sometimes with factories where the prisoners were sent to work. They encountered civilians on their way to the factories and many civilians were used as "guards" in the factories themselves. *Bob* received a kindness from one of those civilian workers. He told me, "There were about six of us sitting there. It was lunchtime. And the guard was there. Not all guards were bad. These were old guards, probably in their 70s, and they were just there to watch us. And he had a sandwich. So you can talk a little bit of German after a while. I said to him, 'Essen?' It means 'eat.' And he said, 'No I can't do that; they see me giving you food they're liable to shoot me.' But when he got up, he left about a quarter of a sandwich there. So I split that between three or four of us. A quarter's not very much of a sandwich, but it was better than nothing, that's for sure, 'cause we didn't eat until we got back about ten hours later."

One of Murray Ebner's work assignments was in a gasoline refinery, repairing damage from bombing runs. He remembers it as a "very cold, ugly place to be at." A civilian German engineer also worked there, and Murray said, "They had a short break and he ate his sandwich. And he was like sitting here, and I was, oh maybe, that far across the way from him. And he seen me observing him. And he said, 'Come over. Come over here.' And he gave me a little piece of his sandwich." Joe Diamond also worked long hours, but in the I.G. Farber factory. Early in his time there, he received a signal from a courageous civilian woman worker who passed near him on the way to the restroom. She would whisper, "Psst!" and point to a low shelf near one of the machines, where she had hidden a sandwich. This went on every day for about two months. Joe believed that the secret extra food provided by this unknown woman helped save his life. And Ben Lohman worked in a nearby copper mine while he was held captive in a Japanese POW camp. The work was physically demanding, especially for the underfed prisoners. Every bit of extra food was highly prized. Ben told me, "An old Japanese man—not a warrior—was in charge of our work crew at the copper mine. One time, he caught a live rabbit and brought it to us as a gift." I bet that rabbit tasted really good to everyone lucky enough to get a bite.

Al's family went into the ghetto when he was ten years old. Two years later, his father was shot by the Germans and his body was thrown into a pit with many others. After hours of searching, *Al's* mother and brother found and identified his father's body by some items in his pockets and brought him home for burial. *Al* described it as the most traumatic experience of his life. Once his family had been transported to a concentration camp, *Al* became one of a number of our survivors who worked in area factories and received secret sandwiches from civilian co-workers. *Al's* sandwich was hidden for him each day by an unknown German woman, in spite of the fact that there were signs everywhere warning the German workers not to communicate with the "inmates." One day, though, a middle-aged German woman passed *Al* on her way to the restroom. She caught his eye and carefully pointed to a box next to the aisle. As soon as he could do so safely, *Al* looked around the box and found a sandwich hidden underneath it, a pattern that continued for a month or so.

He has never forgotten that extended act of kindness: "That lady repeated the noble act of leaving a sandwich for me every day, as long as I worked in that factory. Her righteous deed gave me hope that I no longer possessed, at that time. The pivotal question has been what motivated that German woman to risk her life for me, a stranger. Did she have a son my age, and felt sorry for me? Was she a religious person who tried to abide by the tenets of her faith, to succor the helpless? Did she follow the dictates of her conscience? Was her intention to manifest that not all the Germans were inhumane? Did she wish to assert that under the most ruthless dictatorship, a single human conscience can fight back? Was she just an altruistic person? I shall never know! But I shall forever remember her daring act. She had the conviction and the courage to risk her own life to save another's life, to save someone so very different from herself. She has been and forever will be my heroine (Wiener, 2007)."

Notes

21. www.jewishvirtuallibrary.org refers to this group as the Central Committee of German Jews for Relief and Reconstruction. The group's formation proclamation, dated April 27, 1933, says, in part, "The tasks that await us can only be carried out in unity and cooperation. All our differences of opinion, everything that divides us, must be put aside.

Chapter Six

THE SECOND RESEARCH SURPRISE: SPONTANEOUS INGENUITY

On the evening of my first official interview, I attended a lecture by Benjamin Jacobs, long known as "The Dentist of Auschwitz." Jacobs provided me with the first story of on-the-spot problem-solving that I later came to call "spontaneous ingenuity." The episode that so touched me was his description of him and his father, the last two surviving members of their family, arriving at Auschwitz. They approached the selection table, where a single man made decisions about who would live and who would die. Ben was sent to right-hand line with men fit enough to be workers and his father was sent to the left, which meant the gas chamber. In a moment of confusion, as someone in the next group to approach the selection table tried to make a run for it and was shot, Ben leaped across to the left-hand line, grabbed his father, and jerked him over to the safety of the right-hand line. The deception went unnoticed and both men survived.

In every interview during my four-year odyssey, I had to turn my usual patterns of counseling and therapy completely around. With my clients, I listened as a psychotherapist, engaging in active, often intense, dialogue to work through their issues. As an interviewer, on the other hand, I was a listener with the sole responsibility of creating an environment of trust that let my interviewees feel safe enough to share their stories of survival. The men and women whom I interviewed exhibited a similar adaptability concerning their positive coping skills, developed and refined while they were incarcerated. Somehow, they understood that being a survivor, whether literally or figuratively, is hard work. And somehow, they understood that repetitively grieving the past and/or fearing the future could sap the energy needed to cope with the present.

Every survivor augmented sheer luck with courage, perseverance and the repeated use of the on-the-spot creativity I have come to call "spontaneous ingenuity"—spur-of-the-moment solutions to a problem. Spontaneous creativity calls on pivotal life skills: courage, perseverance and that all-important ability to focus on the moment. My interviews yielded an astounding number of stories that illustrated the concept. This combination of behavioral and emotional patterns, including mental flexibility and a willingness to think outside the box, was something I had seen often during my years as a psychotherapist, though I had not yet found the phrase "spontaneous ingenuity" to describe it. I was surprised to find that prisoners under duress in every setting also used this tool repeatedly to devise solutions to problems large and small, or simply to pass the time—all with the goal of simulating a speck of normalcy in their lives.

Before they were imprisoned, the survivors were like us in many ways. They had choices. They had tried and true methods to solve problems in their daily lives. They knew what tools were available. They equipped themselves with multiple methods of communication and information retrieval. They knew who to contact when they got in over their heads. After they were confined, pervasive uncertainty quickly undermined normality. Problems that were trivial became life-and-death issues. Usual methods of coping and communicating were either too dangerous to utilize or completely unavailable. Choices narrowed. Two of our political prisoners, activists Peng Ming-Min and Ahmed Kathrada, intentionally chose to live with such pervasive uncertainty, but Jews in Central Europe and POWs in every setting had no such choice.

In ways large and small, spontaneous ingenuity played a role in helping all of our survivors figure out how to take some physical, emotional and cognitive control of their situations, thereby helping to manage their stress. Some engaged in deliberate sabotage. Others took advantage of the smallest opportunities to increase their odds of staying alive, driven by an intense need to take action, regardless of the consequences. Each successfully implemented idea—some used only once, others repeatedly—provided a satisfying victory over their captors.

Deliberate Deceptions

The range of deliberate deceptions is broad, starting with a famous escape attempt. Nazi Germany, in addition to forced-labor
camps, transit camps and extermination camps, had an extensive
network of prisoner-of-war camps. The list of "Stalags," as the
German facilities for enemy prisoners were known, is a long one:
41 general camps designated by Roman numerals and letters, six
Stalag Luft camps for captured airmen, one Marlag-Milag camp
for naval and merchant marine prisoners, and four Offlag camps
for ground-force officers. The camps were scattered across Germany, Austria, Czechoslovakia, Poland and Belgium.[22]

At Stalag Luft III, a continuous series of tunneling operations
clearly indicated that the captured troops were trying to follow
the U.S. Army order to do their best to escape and rejoin their
units. The story of the most famous tunnel was told by Paul
Brickhill in The Great Escape, first as a book, then a movie—a
remarkable example of perseverance and creativity. Paul Brickhill, who wrote the book and the screenplay, tells the story with
dexterity and finesse and we are captured by the full gamut of
emotions that led these men literally to lay their lives on the line:
excitement at the idea, fear of discovery, and a desperate determination to get out, no matter the cost. A seemingly innocuous
opportunity afforded them by their Nazi captors—28 minutes a
day during which they could walk freely around a track, talking quietly out of earshot of the guards—enabled the sharing of
secret information vital to the planning process. As *Will* told me,
"The Germans knew we were tunneling, and they knew that we
knew they knew. That opportunity to walk and talk was the most
important of the privileges that they accorded us."

Will got to know the British officer who emerged as the clear
leader of the British and American prisoners in Stalag Luft III
and was the mastermind for a series of escape attempts, many of
them using tunnels. For this latest and largest plan, he carefully
chose specialists to create "tools" for the escapees, and used the
28-minute daily walks to tell them exactly what he needed: 200
forged passes, 200 full outfits of civilian clothes, 200 compasses,
1,000 maps and, for the tunnel itself, railways, air pumps, pipe-
lines and even underground workshops. *Will*, whose father was

a chef, told me he was asked to create a nutritious, concentrated and portable escape food that Brickhill described in detail. The ingredients, scrounged from Red Cross parcels, included sugar, cocoa, Bemax, condensed milk, raisins, oats, glucose, margarine, chocolate and ground biscuits. The mixture was baked into cakes and packed into flat cocoa tins.

After the escape attempt, the commandant of Stalag Luft III was in disgrace and *Will* was among a large group of prisoners transferred to Stalag Luft VII A. He told me that about half the people in the camp thought it was pretty bad but he didn't agree. When he first came to the camp, he started out in a single room with three friends who got shot down before he did. Soon there were six in the room, then ten, then twelve, then sixteen. Barracks that were supposed to hold 300 men held 600. By liberation day, estimates of the camp's population ranged from 80,000 to 100,000.

Pervasive hunger was as common at VII A as at Auschwitz. *Will* told me he weighed 150 pounds when he arrived at VII A and 90 pounds on liberation day. The Germans claimed they were giving the POWs garrison rations but *Will's* senior American officers said that was not the case. He remembers lots of blood sausage, a vegetable they called cow turnips, tiny cans of Spam, and Klim…powdered milk with a backwards name, made in Columbus, Ohio by Borden. (The company sent cases of Klim to a subsequent POW reunion for *Will's* unit.) Six hundred men shared a single stove with a 15-minute time limit per man. Personal items were scarce. *Will* got a toothbrush from a Canadian, a razor from a South African and a greatcoat from an RAF officer. He ordered shoes from home, then got a pair of GI shoes through the Red Cross. He told me proudly, "At liberation, I walked all the way out in those shoes."

The officers at VII A didn't communicate with the guards at all because they didn't want to accidentally reveal any critical information. In a surprise move, though, *Will* actually turned the tables on one of his guards, who casually mentioned that the Germans "have this heavy-water plant in Peenemünde." *Will* knew enough about the science of weaponry to understand what a threat such a plant could be.[23] He told me, "We were sending code back in letters home and we told them, 'You'd better go to Panamundo.'" The message got through. Peenemünde was "blown to smithereens" and the brass in Washington told *Will* to "keep up the good work." *Will* suspected that other prisoners were also sending coded messages home but it wasn't until the 50th reunion of his squadron that he learned who those other people were.

At Stalag VII A, *Will's* group was still able to walk outside together for 28 minutes every day but they were not permitted to interact with other groups of prisoners. But this was a group that never took "No" for an answer. *Will* told me there were a number of Navajo Indians in VII A, at least one of whom was in *Will's* group. The Navajos were able to speak their native language loud enough to be heard on either side of *Will's* walled enclosure. Plans could be made and strategies discussed, with the German guards none the wiser. *Will* told me about the times the Navajos would throw "stuff" over the wire at the top of the dividing wall, then read in Navajo interspersed with English, the latest BBC radio reports.

Like many others, *Ann* worked in a German factory when her family was in the Warsaw Ghetto. She told me, "I worked by Schtrosser Factory. I went through a lot in a couple of weeks because mine machine didn't work. I didn't want to report to the foreman, because he gonna kill me. One evening, that's the only time I gave up on my life. I said to my sister in the evening, 'Tomorrow I'm going to the foreman and tell him about the machine. Either he will fix it, or he gonna kill me. If he gonna kill me, which will be much better because I can't make it any more.'"

The next morning, *Ann* experienced some sheer luck. She was all ready to go to the foreman and tell him about the machine when the door opened and five SS soldiers in the black uniforms came into the factory. They looked at all nineteen girls who were working in the factory and picked *Ann* out of the group. One of the SS men said to her, "You see the table over there with the three [German] ladies? They controlling the bullets. You gonna join them." After he showed *Ann* how to handle the bullets and make sure they didn't have any scratches, she started working with the ladies. She told me, "The bullets come out oily, so I have to clean up and check. And the ladies already went for lunch, but I'm still working and I'm bending down and I see a scratch on the bullet. I stop immediately the machine and I run to the mechanic."

The Nazis had left the management of the factory in civilian hands so Fritz, the mechanic who supervised the crew of women making the bullets, was neither a soldier nor a prisoner. When *Ann* showed him the scratch on the bullet, he took a moment to look around and make sure no Germans were near enough to hear him, and then said, "You know for whom the bullets are going?" *Ann* responded, "For mine brothers and sisters." Fritz said, "I know. I hate what Hitler is doing, killing of innocent people. You know what? I will tell you how you should do it. You gonna sabotage the bullets." *Ann* told me she knew people would think she was crazy for accepting, that the mechanic might have been testing her, might have turned her into the SS for sabotaging the bullets. But *Ann* had been very observant during her time at Schtrosser. She told me, "I accepted so quickly because the foreman always went to Fritz, pointing with his finger and screaming. We're not supposed to listen what he's talking, but one word I picked up, when he said, 'Siberia.' So obviously, Fritz was threatened always with Siberia. That's why I accepted so quickly to sabotage the bullets. My sister had no idea I'm doing that because she would cry, she wouldn't allow me, and it would be a whole thing. But I felt if I can save thousands of people when they pull the trigger and the bullets didn't come out, what is my life and Fritz's life—the two of us—if we can save so many people. So after the war, another girl said, 'I did the same thing you did!' So it just makes me even happier I was not only one."

Charles Brutza found himself deceiving another soldier in order to grant a measure of peace to a dying comrade. Chuck was a U.S. Army medic in Europe during World War II. Under the stress of severe battlefield wounds, many injured soldiers would call out, "Mother! Mother!" Chuck's thoughtful, creative response was to call out just as loudly to his medic-team buddy, like this: "Hey Joe, call this guy's mother and let her know he's OK" or "...let her know where he is." Chuck himself was seriously wounded at one point, and he remembers calling out for his own mother, just as many other men had done before him.

Patrick Hart remembers the family stories about how hard it was in the Japanese internment camp. Rations were one handful of rice per person, per day. His father had to grow everything else and somehow he got seeds for vegetables. Patrick remembers his father being "quite successful" smuggling things in, but everything had to be kept secret. There was a lot of what Patrick called "traitor behavior" among the prisoners in the camp, and he said it was sad that people would do anything to get more rice. Family friends from Manila would throw chickens over the wall at night. Patrick told me, "Until I was eight or nine years old, I didn't know that chicken wasn't actually called 'beans.' My dad educated us that chicken was 'beans' since other families would have snitched on us if they knew."

Remember the torture Marian Haszlakiewicz endured when the Nazis thought he was a member of the Polish Underground? As they mangled his hands, they forced him to give up the names of what they were sure were fellow dissidents during those interrogations. In spite of the pain and the imminent threat of death, Marian kept his wits about him and engaged in a risky charade to feign compliance without giving his captors any valuable information. One by one, he reluctantly gave up names to the SS guards, starting with two men whom he knew had already been shot by the Nazis. Next, he named someone whom he knew had already been arrested. And the fourth name he gave? His own.

Will shared a clever plan that allowed him and his fellow prisoners to obtain first-hand access to incoming mail. He proposed to the guards in charge of unloading the numerous Red Cross packages that he and a few other prisoners would be glad to take over that job. Cigarettes, especially, were highly prized items and were used as currency among the prisoners in the camp. *Will* told me, "We had German guards there to oversee the trucks when they came in from Switzerland. Then a prisoner would say, 'Well, you know, we've been working pretty hard and I think we ought to have a cigarette.'" Since prisoners were not permitted to have their own matches or lighters, they would ask the guards to light their cigarettes. While the guards were distracted by the task, other prisoners would quickly toss some of the select parcels, especially ones with radios or money, into a separate pile.

Michael Stroff told me that almost a hundred tunnels were dug in their camp, though he didn't know of anyone who actually escaped. Every single tunnel attempt yielded quantities of incriminating loose dirt that somehow had to be disposed of. Michael said, "The tunnel-diggers made themselves false pockets, little bags with drawstrings. They would pull the drawstrings when they were walking around on the parade ground to slowly empty out the dirt they'd dug out of the tunnel." Michael also told me about the "Escape and Evasion" kits that were issued to every paratrooper. Each kit contained a tiny compass, a steel file, first-aid equipment, aerial photographs, maps drawn on silk, morphine pills, chewing gum, instruments for the imitation of animal sounds at night, known as "crickets," and a small amount of the local currency of the target country. Even after he was captured, Michael managed to hang onto his small escape-and-evasion hacksaw blade. "I hid the blade in the finger of my glove. I went through three total checks/searches. Since we had to strip down for a full-body search in our birthday suits, I just threw my gloves on the pile of clothes that had already been searched."

Corwin Morey was a devout Catholic. He and a Catholic friend succeeded in creating a forbidden religious icon in plain sight of their captors, using the simplest of materials. In a clearing near their POW camp, the two men laid out a large circle of stones and quietly walked around the circle every day. Doing so eased their minds, and that time was very special to both of them. The Japanese guards never disrupted the walking because they never figured out that the ring of stones was being used as a rosary. Finally, little *Ann* had the simplest idea of all: "I'm short, so I was always among the tall girls, hiding. And I was never hit."

Communicating

Survivors who were deprived of any opportunity for interpersonal support felt that lack deeply. It is not surprising, then, that the most frequent instances of spontaneous ingenuity centered on a compelling need for prisoners in solitary to communicate with each other. Ahmed Kathrada described the process of figuring out ways to converse when he said, "An idea can emerge in a moment. Getting from the idea to the implementation may well take much longer, but the finished 'product' is then a permanent tool of communication among the prisoners." He had a twinkle in his eye when he told me that devising creative ways to communicate was every bit as satisfying as the communication itself: "Well, there is always a sense of satisfaction when you have scored against the enemy. The enemy is trying to do anything possible to try to thwart establishment of communication, so you have to be one better in everything. There's always that feeling of satisfaction."

The Robben Island prisoners engaged in one long-term deception that affected not only them but the world at large. The centerpiece of the idea was Nelson Mandela's autobiography, which he wrote over the course of the first ten years of his more than twenty-five years in prison. The question was how to protect it and how to get it out to the rest of the world. The solution was to copy the original document in tiny letters on almost 600 pieces of very thin paper. One of the political prisoners in the Rivonia group of activists had been a professional tailor before being imprisoned. Using his skill at making tiny stitches, he was able to construct a book in which to hide Mandela's autobiography, packing a copy of the manuscript tightly into the covers of what then looked like a padded photo album. Robben Island officials found and confiscated the original manuscript but, in 1976, the hidden copy was smuggled out of the prison by one of the Rivonia group who was released early (Kathrada, 2000).

Before Kathrada and his fellow prisoners were permitted to actually speak to each other face-to-face, they developed a remarkable variety of ways to pass information amongst themselves. For example, smoking was common among the Robben Island prisoners and guards in the 1960s. As a result, small boxes of matches were often seen around the prison. The boxes provided a quick and easy way to pass around messages. Kathrada said, "So, you know, one would go either to the prison hospital or, when they come to deliver food, the matchbox would just be sitting there, innocuously, and the other side would know that this was a message." After they got out of solitary, the men were granted some outdoor exercise time. "There were times when the colleagues in the communal cells would be sort of playing with tennis balls. The ball would just come over the wall, and the authorities would not know that there was a little slit in the ball. We'd retrieve a message, and put a message back."

Patrick Hart was only six months old when his family was forced into a Japanese internment camp in Manila. The family memories he shared with me during our interview had been repeated so often in the years since the war that they had become lore. From everything Patrick told me, it is obvious that his father's skill at solving problems on the fly kept the family safe until they were liberated. Confined in the camp and unable to communicate with the outside world, Patrick's father made the most of every opportunity to provide for his family, and Patrick told me, "Friends from outside the walls would throw messages over the wall in the middle of the night. My father had a special spot that he watched."

James found his own satisfaction in outwitting his guards with the simplest of acts. While he was being held by the East German Stasi police, the only other person he ever saw was his cellmate (who he later learned was an observer for the Stasi). Each day, *James* had two exercise periods—one in the morning, one in the afternoon—in a private walled space that offered room to walk around but no view of any other areas. As he took his solitary walks each day, he soon realized that he heard what sounded like footsteps in an adjoining area. After concluding that another prisoner was on the far side of the wall, *James* began to figure out how to communicate with him. Finally, he picked up a small pebble in his exercise pen and tossed it over the wall. Nothing. Again, he tossed a pebble over. Again, nothing. Then, a small pebble came flying over the wall from the other side, landing on the ground near him. It wasn't a letter, not even a single sentence. It wasn't a cry for help. These two prisoners were simply sending each other a clear message: "I am here, and now I know that you are here, too."

Bill's extensive injuries had his Viet Cong guards convinced that he was harmless, unable to participate in schemes of any sort. *Bill* thought no such thing, and told me, "We'd take turns doing the dishes, and we would stack the bowls and put a note in the bottom and roll it up real thin so they wouldn't see it. It looked almost like a straw. And we'd send it back through and they would read it. We'd each read it, and we'd know what was going on. It would take a while to do it, and we'd have somebody looking out and making sure the guard wouldn't come."

As World War II drew to a close, the Japanese personnel in Dick Mann's POW camp always had an American radio station playing in the camp kitchen. The Americans delivering food to their fellow prisoners had the luxury of hearing American news reports, in English, and that made them the best sources of news about the war. "The kitchen helpers, they were our people and they are the ones that deliver your food right outside your door. You don't get to see them, but when you know they're coming, you get your ear right down there and they'll have maybe just one little sentence, like 'Russia declared war.'" Dick especially remembers wondering what in the world an "atomic bomb" was, when the news was delivered to him about those events.

In the military prisons of North Vietnam, few if any of the American prisoners had the opportunity to talk face-to-face with each other. Many of the Hanoi Hilton prisoners had served together for a long time. They were used to pooling their expertise to make the best decisions under combat conditions, and had carefully nurtured routines of interpersonal support. But they knew they would likely be put in solitary with no access to their usual methods of communication, and the advent of the tap code meant none of them would have to make it through prison camp alone.

When they were first captured and not yet separated and put in solitary confinement, Bob Shumaker joined forces with three of his fellow prisoners to create the famous Vietnam War "Tap Code." Their accomplishment is an amazing example of spontaneous ingenuity growing out of the intensity of the need, but the story isn't confined to the Vietnam War. In the course of my research, I discovered a unique connection between Bob Shumaker and another of my interviewees, Claude Watkins. Each was a pilot, Bob with the Navy and Claude with the Air Force. Each was a POW, in wars more than thirty years apart. Claude was captured in Germany, eighteen months before the end of World War II. In his POW camp, he learned about the AFLQ tap code used by prisoners to communicate with each other, in spite of being forbidden to do so. Twenty years later, Claude had retired from the service and was working for the Department of Defense as an instructor at officers' survival school. The old AFLQ code was not in the approved curriculum, but Claude would refer to it in his classes as an example of communicating in captivity. In frequent after-class coffee sessions with his students, he was often requested to share more details of the code. One of those students was *Smitty*, a navy captain, who filed AFLQ away in his brain.

Not long afterwards, in 1965, *Smitty* became a prisoner of war in Vietnam, confined in the infamous Hanoi Hilton. His ranking officer was Lieutenant Commander Bob Shumaker, and *Smitty* became one of a group of four officers working to figure out a way of communicating if they were split up. *Smitty* pulled up his memory of the survival-school story of AFLQ, and the four men used AFLQ as the basis for what became known as the Vietnam Tap Code.

The first tapping sent to a new prisoner through the wall would be taps of the old rhythmic phrase, "Shave and a haircut, two bits!" Hearing the taps quickly got the prisoner on the other side of the wall interested in what was going on. The first prisoner would continue to send the pattern of taps until they were sent back to him. After the initial connection was made, the "teacher" began to introduce the concept of a 25-square grid, with "C" doing double duty as both "c" and "k." Letters were identified first by the Row number, then the Column number, and acronyms were common time-savers. For example, a standard message closer was

"God Bless You," or GBU, tapped out as 2-2, 1-2, 4-5. Another common phrase was "Don't let the bedbugs bite"—DLTBBB.

A	B	C	D	E
F	G	H	I	J
L	M	N	O	P
Q	R	S	T	U
V	W	X	Y	Z

Prisoners also used the tap code outdoors, tapping messages with a shovel while appearing to work. Some even sent messages while washing their clothes, snapping the wet clothes in the rhythm of the taps. Eventually, sophisticated offshoots of the tap code were developed, based loosely on the types of visual signals used by coaches at every baseball game. Hubbell described it this way: "A man walking through a courtyard to a bath area could send a short message as clearly as a third-base coach. He knew many pairs of American eyes would be fastened on him, looking for a message and he might want his compatriots to know that so far had been able to hold out against pressure to make an antiwar statement. So he would scratch his head, which meant Row One, then his shoulder, which meant Column Three and the letter would be C; scratch his shoulder which meant Row Three, and his elbow, which meant Column Four, and the letter "O"; scratch his shoulder, Row Three, and touch his toe, Column Five, letter P, and so on until he had spelled out the word c-o-p-i-n-g. In the vermin-infested prison, the guards saw nothing at all unusual in all this scratching; they also were constantly picking and scratching at their own problems.

"The guards also coughed, cleared their throats and spit a great deal, with no idea that when their prisoners did the same thing they usually were talking to each other. One cough was equivalent to one tap; two coughs to two taps; clearing the throat to three taps; a cough and spit to four taps; clearing the throat and spitting to five taps. Sometimes, especially when a prisoner was being taken to or from an interrogation and the others wanted to buck him up or wanted information, like "Are you okay?" or "Any torture?", the amount of coughing, throat clearing and spitting that went on seemed too much even for the rheumiest guards and they could not get out of the cellblock fast enough (Hubbell, 1976)."

Bob emphasized the necessity of tapping quietly and carefully on the prison walls because if the guards caught anyone at it, the reprisals were harsh. He told me, "The way you'd get caught would be that the cells, which were all concrete cells, had a wooden door, and the door itself had a T-patch on it. So the guards, from the outside, could jump to this T-patch and spring it open and look to see if you were communicating. So you got to be pretty crafty. We were able to amplify the sound by taking our little metal cups that were enameled and we'd put them against our ear and against the wall and tap very, very softly. And then, we would be reading the shadows under the door and, you know, if there was any change to the pattern, it meant a guard was near and we'd get off the wall."

Bill and Marian Haszlakiewicz each were also "on the wall," also almost 30 years apart. *Bill* again took advantage of his guards' laxity, and told me, "They came in a couple of times and put somebody in solitary. They didn't do it to me, because they didn't think I would try to tap. But, hey, I was laying right against a wall, so why not? They would tell me what to tap, and it wasn't that hard to learn the code." Marian tapped using Morse Code on plumbing pipes in the communal room he shared with eleven other men. Not only was this useful to other prisoners who had access to a pipe in their own crowded rooms, but the tapped messages also could be heard by prisoners in the room below or above.

Constant Hunger

As odd as it may sound, it was commonplace in every setting to pass the time by thinking about food in order to take your mind off the fact that there was so little of it. Judith Altmann and her fellow prisoners would pretend to cook. "We were sitting and we were 'cooking.' We sort of were making all kinds of things, and that we thought would give us some kind of satisfaction of hunger." Telling me this story reminded Judith of Thereisenstadt, a "model" camp in Czechoslovakia, presented to Red Cross officials as a "real" concentration camp. The Germans even built a swimming pool to help convince the visitors that prisoners were being well-treated. In reality, after the visitors departed, many Jews who were held there temporarily as "model" prisoners were then shipped to Auschwitz or one of the other death camps and were never heard of again. Several of the women held at Theriesenstadt created a small cookbook containing recipes they shared with each other in daily conversations. Many of those women died before they could be liberated but some of the survivors saw to it that this true account was preserved. In a personal connection to the Theresienstadt cookbook, I attended a Holocaust memorial service a few years ago at the Synagogue in New Albany, Ohio. My former colleague, Cheryl Meisterman, had a copy of the Theresienstadt cookbook, In Memory's Kitchen, and the two of us took cookies, made from one of the book's recipes, for a reception after the service.

Larry Bott could have been speaking for every prisoner in every setting when he told me that food rations, minimal at best, became even more meager as the war neared its end. He entertained me with a brief lesson on how to survive on Army WWII K-rations: "for breakfast, take out the Nescafe, sugar and fruit bar and throw everything else; for lunch, eat the canned cheese and throw everything else; for dinner, keep the toilet paper and the chocolate bar and throw the rest, particularly the can of corned pork loaf with apple flakes. By all means, keep a waxed box to burn like a candle and heat a canteen of water for coffee in your foxhole, without smoke."

Several prisoners made tiny cook stoves out cans, and Sonia Mentelmacher used a can she found to smuggle food into the camp: "I made holes in a can, it should be like a grater. I grate up potatoes and I put them here in a little bag, between my legs. It was easier to get it in that way. They wouldn't find it, in a little bag, you know, under the clothes." *Harry* ended up in a POW camp for British officers and use his creative bargaining skills to get extra food. He told me, "On a daily basis, I had to learn to get along with the British group I was in. I still had a watch and a fountain pen, and even though I never smoked I always took my share of any cigarettes. Other prisoners would offer me food in exchange for my possessions and I was a very good trader. 'Food' was starvation rations, black bread with sawdust in it (hard to digest!) and green soup. I lost weight and got night blindness."

The stealing of food was also common, and Dick Mann shared a story with me about tomatoes. He and his buddy, Derocher, knew that their Japanese guards were cultivating tomato plants. As they tried to figure out how to steal some of the tomatoes, they quickly concluded that any attempt had a better chance of success if it happened at night, in the shadows of moonlight. They never took any red tomatoes because they knew the guards checked their vines every day to see how red the fruit was. But Dick and Derocher had a regular supply of green tomatoes and even ate the stems whenever they got one. Once they had stuffed the pockets of their flight suits with tomatoes, they had a lookout who helped them get safely back to their cells.

Murray Ebner told me a story that beautifully illustrates the extreme risks taken by prisoners, families or friends of prisoners, and even some guards to make things a little easier for the prisoners: "This was a place which was built, I don't know, maybe five or six years before the war, a house managed by Polish wardens. Now, when the Germans took over, they replaced only the officers, heads of the prison. And the wardens doing some physical management in the prisons were the same guys who used to be before the war. We were in an unusual situation. In the cell next door there were no discussions whatsoever because people were so hungry and weak. My cell was a privilege, because the underground and our families bribed the Polish wardens and smuggled food through to this eleven or twelve happy individuals. Those Polish wardens risked their lives doing so. Whatever money they got for this service, it is in no relationship to their risk, because if anybody talked, they are dead immediately. [The Nazis] were merciless in cases like that."

Maintaining Mental Discipline

The importance of maintaining mental discipline as a stress-management tool cannot be overstated. There are no hard and fast rules about how to keep your mind in shape; any structured activity pattern can become a deliberate diversion from the stresses of the moment. As a career Navy man and therefore an expert in structured activity patterns, Bob Shumaker understood the advantages of maintaining mental discipline, even in the POW camp. He and his group devised a mental database of Allied personnel in their camp, with the intention of passing it along to their superiors once they had been freed. Bob said, "We thought it was important to carry out this body of knowledge [of who was dead, who was alive, who was in the camp with us], especially if we were successful in escaping. We would have memory lists. In order for a person to enter our database, they had to have been seen by another person; there had to be two sources. And so every day we would go over the lists. They got pretty lengthy. Initially you think, gee, it's like memorizing the telephone book, but most of us at the time could spit right through this list of five hundred, not only names but shoot-down dates and circumstances."

It is almost impossible to believe, but Thaddeus Stabholz was able to continue the mental discipline of medical studies in the Ghetto. He told me, "I had two years of medical school, before the war, at Warsaw University, and in the ghetto was underground medical school. And I attended as much as I could for almost two years. There were medical students from before, at regular medical school. There were a few professors who just carry on, lectures and so on. It was very difficult, because we were all hungry, we had to work in the hospital, and sometimes the lectures were at 2:00 in the morning in a cold room, because it was an underground school, and if somebody would be arrested by a German, he would be tortured to find out, because all kinds of higher education was tricky."

Ahmed Kathrada described another ingenious way of maintaining mental discipline among the prisoners on Robben Island. To keep their minds occupied while their bodies did hard labor breaking up gravel, they developed the idea of having their own university. Kathrada told me, "When we went to work, not only did they allow us to talk, but they allowed us to work in groups. The work was very difficult in the beginning. None of us had done pick-and-shovel work in our lives, and every day there were blisters and bleeding hands. But there were also the advantages of being outside. Once we got used to the work, it was less difficult, and while we were working, we could be studying without paper. Fortunately among us were teachers, historians, English teachers. There were two medical doctors, proficient in the sciences. I did history, with my 'colleagues' gathered around me doing lessons and discussing."

Curtis Brooks exercised his own mental discipline to hone a life skill during his time in the Japanese internment camp. He said, "We were always vastly interested in whatever news we could get, progress of the war. For quite a long time we got the Japanese-controlled English-language Manila daily paper, their propaganda sheet. We became very adept at reading that, reading between the lines, interpreting what was said and what wasn't said. You learned to x-ray ideas and find out what skeleton of truth lay underneath the padding of whatever fluff was put out. I think that was a skill we developed almost unconsciously, and it stays with me yet."

Passing the Endless Hours

It was common in concentration camps, POW camps and Robben Island for prisoners to have occasional moments of free time. Many of them would occupy their minds by planning and implementing a wide variety of diversions, such as old, familiar games. Prisoners' pre-war activities, as well as their military skills, influenced the direction of their thoughts. For example, if you had been a bridge player or a poker player at home, you'd want to find a way to play cards in your camp. Albert Allan and his buddies passed the time by playing poker and bridge with handmade cards, but Albert learned early on to be careful. He told me, "Yes, I got in, but I learned my lesson really quick. I lost some buns in the poker game. We used to get bread maybe once or twice a week, and I lost them once!"

Dick Mann was an avid checkers player, as were many of his fellow prisoners. He said, "We tried to make a checkerboard. We got certain kinds of rocks and we worked like heck to get them, you know? They had to be different and yet the same in a way. We finally got the thing all set and were going to have a game with the guys who had worked the hardest, and the guards came out there and kicked all the stones away. [A little laugh.] You know, if you'd been in your own country and had a little protection, you know, you'd take care of something like that, but there was nothing you could do."

The men in Bob Shumaker's group excelled at innovation and figured out a number of different ways to use their tap code. Bob remembered, "We had these mosquito nets that were finely woven, but about every inch was kind of a heavy line, their reinforcement line. You'd normally use it at night, but in the daytime, you could fold it to make a chessboard with eight rows and eight columns. Then you'd take toilet paper (I mean this isn't any toilet paper that you could recognize as such) and make little markings where we'd fold. So maybe triangles would mean the pawns, for example. Chess was usually reserved for Sundays, when the guard force would go down a little bit because a single game could take eight hours or so."

Will played a supporting role in the Great Escape. Because he did not draw one of the 200 places on the list of those who would try to escape, list, he never got to see if his idea actually worked. He and the others covertly watched with the other non-escapees while seeming to go about their regular routines. Seventy-six men escaped, but they were slowly rounded up, one by one. After two weeks, only three men were still free, all of whom eventually made it to England (Brickhill, 1950). Stress levels among all the prisoners spiked when they watched the escapees discover that their tunnel surfaced a few terrifying yards short of the safety of the nearby forest. Most made it to freedom, but two were shot dead as they exited the tunnel.

An offshoot of the tunnel planning was acquiring knowledge about what was going on in the outside world. It turned out to be incredibly simple for the men to get the latest news. *Will* told me, "So we said, 'Can we buy newspapers?' Much to our amazement, they said yes. So we took several German newspapers. These fellows who spoke perfect German, they'd read it, and then they would translate and they'd tell us how many airplanes they'd shot down. And they always exaggerated. What we did, we took the tonnage of sinkings by U-boats, and we took it from 1939 to the present, and it kept diminishing. That's how we predicted the end of the war."

Being able to think outside the box was an important skill, and the men in *Will's* group were very good at it. He said, "Didn't make any difference what the hell it was, but every week we had the 'Idea Club.' One might be how to get out of prison. Two might be what to do when you got home. We had all kinds of things. And that was a very interesting bunch of people that we had. We used to say, 'Anything you can think of that needs to be done, you can find somebody in here who's probably able to do it.' We had a watch repairman. We had a tailoring department. We had a 'goods' department, which is what I was doing, limited as it was. At one point, they were making compasses out of phonograph records and we needed a little glass in there to cover the needle, so it wouldn't get wet. So I said, 'How do you get glass?' The guy looks over there and says, 'Huh. Got a window in there?' He knocked the window out and then he said, 'Well you know what you can do is, you can cut glass underwater with ordinary scissors.' I don't know where he got that, but I watched him do it. Not real ice cold, but just cool water. He said, 'It absorbs the shattering and you can go around there.'"

Others familiar with electronics used their skills to build secret radios, a common activity in POW camps. Charles Mott was one of many prisoners from aircraft crews who possessed the necessary engineering knowledge to know what was needed, and the skills to put it all together. Finding the component parts occupied a lot of time, a bonus in itself. Charles told me, "It doesn't take much to build a radio. We could use a crystal or vacuum tubes, and we had some very well-qualified guys. You could pick up Indiana and, in some cases, San Francisco. Of course, the news was dismal the first six months of the war."

Everyday Activities

Several survivors told me about figuring out how to accomplish the kind of simple, everyday activities that you and I take for granted. Take smoking, for example, which almost everyone did during WWII. A cigarette was an uncommon treasure for Dick Mann and his fellow prisoners in the Japanese POW camp, but the cost to get hold of one could be strange indeed: "Everybody smoked back then, and the only way you could get a cigarette was to kill and turn in a hundred dead flies. And that's a lot of flies! So we were able to make sort of a fly swatter out of a piece of bamboo. And there were three of us who really liked to smoke, so we had a team. When we'd get a hundred dead flies, we'd go over to the Japanese and make a big ritual out of it, passing it around. Oh, and we made little cigarette holders. So, when somebody got the fire in his mouth, then we knew we needed to go back to the flies again."

Creative problem-solving covered a wide range of circumstances. Murray Ebner didn't trade dead flies for cigarettes but he figured out how to kill them: "We did something unusual to accomplish a task, like taking out the inside of your shoe to whack a fly." *Will* told me that because there was little or no access to razors and blades in POW camps, he made an important discovery: "You could sharpen the blade in the palm of your hand." *Will* obviously enjoyed the comfort of having a decently sharp razor blade, especially because it was a product of his own ingenuity. For *Hank*, the extreme winters in Germany and Poland, combined with insufficient clothing and starvation diets, meant he and his fellow prisoners were always cold. But *Hank* and his fellow prisoners figured out a solution: "We would grab whatever we could. Sometimes, if we worked around cement bags, where we have the cement for building roads, we'd hide little pieces of paper in our pockets to put in our shoes; it would warm you up a little bit. Sometimes you would take an empty cement bag and shake out all the leavings. There were three layers in those bags. We'd take one layer and cut out the head and the arms and put it over you and put the jacket on top of you. Of course you had to get rid of it before you entered the camp."

Access to a pencil was a rare and unusual treat for anyone in a Nazi prison camp, and both Judith Altmann and Thaddeus Stabholz treasured theirs. Judith said, "I wrote. Whenever I could get a pencil I wrote a little bit, like a diary of fact. It was confiscated when they found it, but it still helped." Thaddeus also made a direct connection between writing and coping with his stress: "Writing has an additional thing, unloading. You had the feeling that your brain was exploding." *Harry* found a way to listen to BBC newscasts and shared what he heard with his fellow prisoners. He told me, "We were able to have meetings and exchange news, which we sometimes received from the BBC radio. We were lucky to have those capabilities." And Larry Bott found a productive way to use his high-school graduation present: "I had the only luminous-dial watch in our platoon. Every night I gave it to guys on two-hour guard duty. They would use it and pass it to the next man, all night long. I still have that watch and once in a while I wind it and listen to it tick. I doubt if I ever will throw it away."

Laughter Really *is* the Best Medicine

This final section on spontaneous ingenuity is all about the benefits of being able to access your sense of humor in times of stress. Being able to laugh in the face of chaos might not save your life, but it could well save your sanity. Imagine being in Curtis Brooks' shoes, stuck in a Japanese internment camp and having to deal with puberty in the middle of a war. He described it this way: "We were going from thirteen to sixteen, a time of change. Thrown in fairly intimately with girls. Go loping along with your knuckles on the ground, baying and howling. I was always very shy about that sort of thing, but nevertheless that kind of interest/ diversion was always present."

Carl Cossin's sense of humor showed up in even the midst of his stress-filled trek to the Korean POW camp. He said, "They took us on across this road into a field of hay stubble and started to march us south. We knew if they had turned north, they would have just shot us. Since they turned south, my buddy, Trent, said, 'Let's take 'im out!' And I said, 'With what?! Take 'im out with what? We got our hands wired behind us. Spitballs?!'"

When asked if there were particular events that were especially helpful in his recovery, Marian Haszlakiewicz couldn't help laughing as he told me about one of his cellmates deciding to teach him to dance as part of the rehabilitation process. Imagine turning a small jail cell, say twelve feet square, "home" to eleven or twelve prisoners, into a dance studio. It was one of the few things that would get everyone laughing out loud. Marian said, "You may laugh, but the most interesting were the dancing lessons! This fellow that took care of my hands and my well-being was also a teacher of dancing. Probably nowhere else, in any prison, did this take place."

By now you are familiar with the constancy of hunger that faced every prisoner. Bob Shumaker puts a humorous light on it with this story: "We'd get two meals a day and it varied quite a bit. But I know, at one time, for three months straight, the diet would be cabbage soup, without much cabbage. It was kind of a broth, you know? So in the middle of this, about 1967 or so, when the Americans were hitting Hanoi pretty hard with bombs, sometimes there would be maybe six or seven attacks a day. One time after we'd been on this cabbage soup for a long time, I recognized the voices of my Naval Academy classmates, shouting from the other side of the prison, which was kind of unusual, because we learned not to say anything. They were shouting, over and over, as if they were talking to the Americans in their bombing run, 'Bomb the cabbage patches!' We started tapping on the pipes during air raids with the same message: 'Bomb the cabbage patches!'"

Notes

22. www.merkki.com/powcampsmap.htm
23. For more information about heavy water, see www.pbs.org/wgbh/nova/hydro/water.html

Chapter Seven

POST-LIBERATION:
SHADOWS OF THE BARBED WIRE

You will better understand the feelings associated with the various liberations days if I set the stage with one survivor's description of the bleakness of captivity: "The prisoner, if he's incarcerated for six months or five years in prison or no parole or something, at least you have a time when you expect to get out. As a prisoner of war, you have no idea. You just don't throw anything away. You try as best you can to take care of your health, but you have no idea when it's going to end. You don't know even whether it's going to end. You have no future. You have no deadline."

Now, contrast this with Liberation Day. No matter how much anyone speculated about what it would be like, when it came, it was almost too much to take in. Each survivor had a lot of time to reflect on it, to daydream about it. Some of them were too weak to even react. Many were overcome by the abundance of food that was offered to them by the liberating forces. When the emotional state of captivity described gave way to a liberation day that was always hoped-for but never a certainty, many survivors' reactions could hardly be contained.

Albert Allen's memories of that day are still vivid: "We saw a B-24 and another smaller plane come over and drop a bunch of men. The Japanese guard was running around saying, 'War is over!'" Because Albert's POW camp was in the middle of Manchuria, its liberation came much later than that of many other camps. The men knew the Russians were finally fighting the Japanese and they were fearful of what that might mean, especially since they watched the Japanese digging pits around the camp, preparing to kill all the prisoners. Albert said, "So that was a big moment, finally seeing that bomber come over. And they opened up the door and flew an American flag on the side. The next thing, we saw another one come over and bank, and we saw these parachutes—different colors, blue, green and white—and there were six men: a Japanese interpreter, a Chinese interpreter, and four American CIA."

Albert told me the men parachuting down almost got executed right there when they hit the ground: "A Japanese officer saved them when he ran over and told his guards, 'Don't hurt any of these men. Take them down to the hotel in the middle of town. The war's over with.'" The ranking American officer in the camp, a major general, went to town to talk with the men who had parachuted in. He came back to camp and told us that even though the U.S. had stopped fighting, the Russians had not and no peace treaty had been signed, meaning the prisoners would have to wait for the fighting to stop before they could be airlifted out. In spite of their frustration and disappointment about the delay, Albert remembers that two days later, the food got better, making the waiting a little easier to take.

Hank's Nazi guards had taken everyone from his barracks out into the woods, but nobody knew why. They were sitting in a circle and could hear bombing and shooting getting closer and closer. They all looked up at the sound of some low-flying aircraft, and when they looked back down, all their guards had disappeared. *Hank* had been conditioned not to trust anything, and warned his buddies not to run away: "If you decide to escape, they'll kill you. So, none of us moved. We stayed because we knew maybe it was a hoax, although they didn't need an excuse to kill you. If they don't like your looks and they feel like killing someone, they didn't care. So we stayed."

They could never have imagined what happened next: "All of a sudden, out of nowhere, a big tank came over. We could see the highway and I see they kept coming toward us, coming toward us. And all of a sudden, we said, 'Uh-oh, they've got lots of ammunition to kill us. What is this tank doing here?' We didn't know. But there was, thank God, an American. It was an American tank and a soldier jumped out, off the tank. His parents came to the United States a long time ago and he knew a few words in Polish, so he was picked to talk to us. He kept saying 'America! America!' And then he said, in Polish, 'You're free!!!'" This was their dream, come true. *Hank* said, "And, oh my God! We were set free! We didn't have any tears for that right there! All we have is happiness! Then, we cried. And then they gave us food. You never saw so much food. We all ate too much, too fast and then were holding our stomachs, groaning. The American soldier got on the radio to call somebody, medics or something. Then came two guys in a jeep with a red cross on it. They gave us all medicine and told us we had to eat more slowly."

Harry's group had been moved to Moosberg, where they could be out in the sun during the day and watch the British bombers come over at night. Flak was bouncing off the roof and the buildings, and one bomb came so close to their compound that the concussion moved a wall away from the floor. Harry described it for me: "Liberation Day, my goodness! A tank came into the compound, ran over the main gate. We saw the muzzles of cannon. I just happened to be looking out over Moosberg. The Nazi tent was down. I saw the Nazi flag come down. Old Stars and Stripes went up."

When Adrienne Krausz was 20 years old, she and everyone from her town were held in Altenburg before an overnight "death march." Everyone was told to bring their belongings, which at this point consisted of only a coat and whatever they were wearing. Each person got a half-loaf of bread. They marched all night, and anyone who couldn't keep up was killed. The next day, they arrived in the small town of Weldenburg, Saxony, and were told to simply sit on the pavement in the town square, in the rain. They each got another half-loaf of bread that afternoon. After they ate, their guard led them up a hill to a forest area. Adrienne remembers hearing lots of activity, "airplanes, bombs and everything." Nobody knew what was happening, but nobody dared challenge the SS guards or the Nazi soldiers with their big German shepherds. They were told to stay there overnight, lying in the mud, in the rain.

Adrienne told me, "In the morning, when it starts to be light and you woke up, there was quiet. And then we started to hear cars moving and big trucks and everything, and the soldiers disappeared. Some of the Wehrmacht, regular army, a few of them even came up to some of the men, pointing a revolver, and said, 'You should say that I was always good to you.'" Still not knowing what was happening, the group of prisoners, now minus the threatening presence of their guards, took action. Adrienne continued the story: "So we got two or three men from our group to go down to town, and there came shout from town, 'Come on down! The Johnnies are here! The American Army.' And, my God, they showered us with chocolate and with other candies. I didn't even mind they hit me in the head with the candies. From tanks and cars, was a motorized unit. Friday, April 13, 1945. I'm glad. I just wish it would have happened to the entire family, that I wouldn't have been the only one."

By early February 1945, the Russians were approaching Claude Watkins and Stalag Luft IV on the drive that eventually took them to Berlin and victory. The prisoners were given a few days' notice that most of them would be moved by foot to another camp, described only as "a few days to the west." They departed on February 6 in groups of approximately two hundred. Captivity conditions immediately changed drastically. Claude's group stayed relatively intact, spending eighty-six days on the road, walking, as Claude put it, "route step and under guard" for fifty-seven of them. When the men weren't marching, they stayed in barns or outdoors in fields or on the roadside. They then took a 165-mile trip packed into boxcars and, at its conclusion, spent twelve days in a huge tent in a corner of Stammlager XI-A near Altengrabow, a camp that, as Claude said, "seemed to hold captives of all western nationalities."

After this break, his group resumed their trek and continued walking until they were liberated at Bittefeld on April 26, following negotiations the previous evening between the Wehrmacht Captain in charge of all the groups of POWs in that area and representatives of the 104th US Infantry Division. Claude told me, "At the time, American forces were approximately 15-20 miles to the west of us and Soviet forces about the same distance to the East. It probably took very little thinking on the part of the German Captain to decide who he should surrender to." Claude said that knowing liberation was getting closer each day was probably the main thing that sustained them all during the almost three-month-long migration. He still felt the emotion when he told me, "Liberation! Just the word itself denotes freedom, but it must be long and hopefully awaited, anticipated, and then finally realized, for it to have its full, almost indescribable meaning. Liberation. The good guys came and took you away from the bad guys. Your country had the will and its military had the initiative, the guts and the ability to kick butt and win! To get you and all the marbles."

Ahmed Kathrada had a different kind of liberation-day moment at the sentencing hearing in the Rivonia Trial of Nelson Mandela and his associates. The men weren't being freed from prison, but rather were freed from the specter of execution, so their unique "liberation day" was actually the first day of twenty-seven years of captivity. Kathrada described the scene: "At the time of our arrest, more or less from day one, the thought jumped into our heads that we would be sentenced to death. Right until this period of isolation ended, we were also told, 'Prepare for the worst.'" The case had lasted for about nine months and for that entire time, the expectation of death never left the men. Finally, the day came when the judge took the bench and instructed them to stand up and hear their sentence. Kathrada continued, "When he said, 'Life sentence,' it was collective relief. Our supporters throughout the trial had the same stresses we did, fearing a death sentence for us all. They obviously had the same relief on hearing the life sentence, because a great cheering filled the very crowded courtroom. We were all grinning!"

Post-Traumatic Stress Disorder

Liberation Day may have marked release from the horrors of captivity for our survivors, but this was no fairy-tale ending. While they were prisoners, none of my interviewees had had either recourse or resources to defend against the treatment they received, and all of them suffered through traumatic stresses. Liberation, therefore, actually signaled the beginning of years, even decades, of coping with the aftermath of those traumatic stresses. For many years, the medical community had no real understanding of the effects of such high levels of stress. From the Civil War through World War I through Vietnam, such severe trauma was diagnosed initially by military medical personnel as "soldier's heart" (Civil War), "shell shock," (WWI), "battle fatigue" or "combat fatigue" (WWII) and "post-Vietnam syndrome" (Vietnam).

One hundred twenty years after the Civil War, a definitive diagnosis finally emerged. After reviewing more than a century of studies into battle veterans' post-conflict symptoms, researchers finally had been able to identify and name Post-Traumatic Stress Disorder (PTSD), thereby superseding the vague descriptions of their symptoms that had plagued veterans for so long: disturbed sleep, nightmares with sudden wakening, emotional tension, anxiety and flashbacks (the vivid re-living of a traumatic experience, whether waking and sleeping). The researchers found that, after the original traumatic event, stress deepens into traumatic stress in the presence of an extremely severe reaction to an event or events intense enough to overwhelm our psychological and physiological resources. In short, post-traumatic stress disorder is the sum of the reactions that follow the initial hurt or harm or trauma (DSM-IV, 1994). At last, it had become clear to medical personnel that the veterans who had been repeatedly subjected to the horrors of war were not mentally ill, as had been thought. Rather, they were enduring flashbacks—intense episodes of "reliving" combat when awake (DSM-IV, 1994). Such flashbacks are an immediate reaction to a "trigger," i.e., an event, smell or sound, seemingly unrelated to the original traumatic experience, which has the power to evoke it instantly. Episodes can also occur during sleep, though those are more likely the result of accumulated unconscious triggers.

In Korea and Vietnam, the use of helicopters was common by American forces. Many soldiers who had served in those conflicts experienced frightening flashbacks after returning to the U.S. if a helicopter with its unique sound was within earshot. In fact, the sound of helicopters or the visual pattern of the turning rotors is so often a PTSD trigger, that the National Institutes of Health conducted a 1992 study: An evaluation of the impact of "helicopter ride therapy" for in-patient Vietnam veterans with war-related PTSD.[24] Symptoms of post-traumatic stress include disturbed sleep, nightmares with sudden wakening, emotional tension, anxiety and flashbacks, all examples of the "replay loop" mentioned earlier. Treatments, as documented by the Mayo Clinic, including medications (antipsychotics, antidepressants, anti-anxiety medications and prazosin), psychotherapy (cognitive therapy, exposure therapy, and eye-movement desensitization and reprocessing, EMDR), and acupuncture.[25]

Multiple traumatic stresses are readily apparent in each of the following stories, as are the survivors' efforts to deal with the after-effects—the PTSD—for years after being liberated. For example, *Hans'* family was Dutch. He was born in 1934 in Java, located in the island group formerly known as the Dutch East Indies. His parents were missionary teachers and his father later was ordained as a minister and assigned to the Dutch Reformed Church in Singapore. That city was bombed the same day as Pearl Harbor and the family fled back to Java. Soon after the bombing, the islands were taken over by the Japanese and all Dutch nationals were rounded up and interned in a series of camps. *Hans'* father was taken to a POW camp; he and his mother, along with his younger brother, were "Guests of the Emperor" in four different internment camps.

When *Hans* turned 11, he was taken from his mother and put in a camp with men. *Hans* remembers the men in the camp as "not particularly good men" and says it was a hellhole. Luckily, he was only there a month or two before the atom bomb was dropped in Japan "and that saved our lives." *Hans* also says he wouldn't have survived without his mother, who was a "tower of strength." He was sustained throughout the war not so much by what his mother said but by what she did. He told me she managed to make a "little home" out of whatever space she and her children had, whether it included walls or not. And even when there was very little food, she made a ritual out of eating. Her wisdom of creating a veneer of normalcy in the midst of chaos served him well. Another habit of his mother's was just as valuable: she talked about the past, which gave *Hans* a sense of being someone, and the future, saying, "This is going to be past at some point, and what are you going to do then?"

Hans and his mother and brother were released by the Japanese in August 1945. They returned to the Javanese city where they had been living before the war and *Hans'* father, who had also survived, found them there. Almost immediately after World War II ended, however, the Indonesians began a war of revolt against the Dutch and by October 1945, the family had been interned once again. Less than a year later, in July 1946, *Hans'* family was freed. The war for independence, which involved sporadic fighting and much international diplomacy, continued for four more years. Finally, under the auspices of the United Nations, based in The Hague, Netherlands, Indonesia's sovereignty over the former Dutch East Indies was recognized on December 29, 1949.

Sixty years ago, when World War II was over, *Hans* was only 12 years old. When I interviewed him in 1996, he had become a psychologist and was able to view his wartime experiences through the lens of that training. His understanding of the differences between his and his brother's traumatic experiences is remarkable. He told me, "The lack of privacy is awful. It's really awful. There's no place to go. It was harder for my little brother, who was five-and-a-half years younger than me, because I was able to articulate things more. So I think for little kids it's harder because they have the internalized experience without being able to put words on it." *Hans* said he could easily see that he had a severe case of post-traumatic stress: "It was quite an affliction because I didn't know what it was. Once I was a professional psychologist, I learned about this. All of a sudden, the lights went on!" I asked *Hans* if there were gaps in his memories due to the extreme stresses. He gave me an answer that had grown out of his professional training: "Not gaps in knowing what went on, but gaps in feelings. Dissociation, as you know, is not that you don't remember, but that you don't remember the feelings. So it's a very helpful coping mechanism, but one that can also become difficult later on. What happened to me was that the feelings came back rushing in."

Thaddeus Stabholz was an only child, born in 1917 in Poland. When the Germans invaded Poland in 1939, Thaddeus was 22 years old and just finishing up his second year of medical school.

He and his family were confined in the Warsaw Ghetto, a small section of the most severely damaged part of the city. Concentrating a population of 400,000 Jews into such a small area caused massive overcrowding, with ten people crammed into rooms meant for one or two. There was no electricity. Hygiene was very poor because the ghetto sewer and water systems had been destroyed by Allied bombing. Lice, typhus and dysentery spread rapidly.

Food was strictly rationed, and food cards were the only means of getting anything to eat. Working Jews were allotted 400 calories a day; non-working Jews got 300. Thaddeus, whose mother had died before the war, watched helplessly as his father succumbed to conditions in the Ghetto. He described it to me this way: "We lived in the ghetto and we thought it cannot be worse. But you know, from day to day it got worse and worse and worse. We thought we were rotting in hell. When you were in a concentration camp, you thought the ghetto was paradise. In concentration camp, I had some help, otherwise I could not survive. I met in Auschwitz some doctor I knew from medical school, who was helping to maintain an underground med school in the Ghetto. Later on in Dachau in 1944 and 1945, it was about the worst time. It was extremely difficult work for German factories in extreme cold, with almost nothing to eat. I was at 77 pounds." The only bright spot in Dachau was when the prisoners saw American planes attacking.

Thaddeus told me he went through those years in an emotional vacuum. "When you were in a concentration camp, you had no energy to feel anything. We knew it eventually would get better but we didn't have enough strength, enough energy to feel anything. Completely emotionally dead." His main goal was just to survive Hitler and see what the world would be like after Hitler was gone. But once that happened and the war was over, the emotional vacuum didn't automatically go away. Thaddeus said he couldn't talk to anyone and thought he was going insane before he finally discovered the therapeutic effects of writing. I interviewed him in 2001, over 50 years after the war. Those intervening years had not lessened the intensity of a nightmare that he had had for many years—an experience that illustrates details may shift, but the theme of the dream persists: "I have PTSD and I always had dreams and the dreams were always similar, that I am going to the gas chamber. They close the locks, the lights turn off, and they throw in the gas and I start suffocating. At the last moment an angel takes me on his body and we fly away. After I was liberated, the dreams were different. I was going to the gas chamber, lights turn off, complete darkness. But then it was no angel. I was suffocating. I would wake up gasping and I was in terror, and my wife didn't know what happened. I didn't want to tell my wife. …It was strange. In Auschwitz, I was saved; after liberation, I was dying!"

Sonia Kofchick Mentelmacher was born in Poland in 1928. She was one of six children, and only three years old when the family was first moved into a ghetto. Three years later, a pattern had been established where ghetto residents were routinely ordered to gather in the middle of the town marketplace. Each time, a group was selected and taken away. During one of those gatherings, when Sonia was 11 years old, she was standing with her mother and her two youngest sisters. When her mother saw the soldiers taking out people, she picked up one toddler, took the other by the hand and pushed Sonia away, saying, "You go away from me! You go to the other side!" Sonia did so, and then watched as her mother and the smaller children were immediately taken away. She never saw them again. Sonia lived because her mother had the strength to make the choice that would give her older daughter a chance to survive.

Memories of the Holocaust still hover over Sonia, so much so that the Holocaust Memorial in Miami makes her uneasy, even after all these years: "When you are in Florida, you go to Miami. They have right over there, on 17th Avenue, behind Jackie Gleason's theater, they have a memorial. I'm not going there anymore. For me, it's very painful. On the courtyard there is statue of a woman with a child, and I see my mother, and I cannot go. I can't see it anymore."

Sonia and her husband, Max, lived their lives on parallel tracks during the war. Max, who was also a child during the Holocaust, was imprisoned in different camps than Sonia. The two met and married after the war. Almost 60 years after Liberation, Max and Sonia still feel the anguish. Max said, "We didn't commit any crime. Just because we happened to be born Jews, that's about all, nothing else." Sonia added, "What did mine little sisters do? They were babies really, both of them, that they took them, that they got burned. What did my father do? In the gas chamber. My mother? A young woman...."

Steve was born in northern Ohio in 1926. He enlisted in the Army at age 17. Before he turned 18, he had been shipped overseas, fought enough battles to feel like a veteran, and was captured by the Germans. He turned 18 in a POW camp in 1944 and was liberated in April 1945; he never shared his experiences with anyone until 1991. For the whole of the intervening 46 years, *Steve* had been going to doctors and being treated for symptoms of PTSD, though back then none of the doctors he saw knew what to call it except battle fatigue. As *Steve* put it, "They all say, 'It all stems back to when you was in the war.'" As luck would have it, *Steve* finally encountered a doctor that could help: "Up in Cleveland at the VA, this doctor worked with me and it took about a year-and-a-half that I could start telling this. Now I'm working with a lot of the other people that have been prisoners of war. Doctor says I'll always have these memories of flashback moments with me." Though the circumstances of each episode differ widely, *Steve* (and everyone who has PTSD) has had to deal with both the unwelcome memories themselves as well as with the realization of how difficult it is to control the reactions to those memories.

Schwangford, Germany was *Steve*' first POW camp and it turned out to be the source of two startling experiences of post-traumatic stress flashbacks. The first began with a seemingly simple event that triggered an intense flashback years after his release. He told me, "The first camp I was in, where I was tortured, was in Schwangford, Germany. Now, I can watch a movie and it won't set me off or nothing, and I can bring everything back to reality. But I had a little incident happen the other day when I had a man come here that was going to do some cement work for me." When *Steve* answered the door, the workman was wearing a shirt that had big letters across the front that read, "Schwangford, Germany." As the two men looked at each other, the workman could tell instantly that something was wrong but he had no way of knowing that *Steve* was experiencing a flashback. When *Steve* told me all this in our interview, he said, "I never had anything just 'oomph!' real fast like that. And I said, 'Where'd you get that shirt!?'" The workman explained that his uncle was in the Army, serving in Schwangford "It's just a shirt," he said. *Steve* said, "No, it ain't! I was a prisoner of war [there] and I don't like nothing that says 'Schwangford, Germany!' Now, I can say it or you could write it and it don't bother me. That day, big bright letters just did it. It took the rest of the day to kind of get myself calmed down. It's just like, when it grabs you, you feel like grabbing hold of somebody and just beating them up or even killing them. You're so tense. You know you couldn't do anything at the time you was a prisoner, but now it's on a different ground. And so it just brings it out all of a sudden. And you wonder sometimes, 'Will I always be this way?'"

The second flashback was triggered by a sound. *Steve* had escaped from Schwangford twice. The first time, he was caught, brought back to camp, and put in the sweatbox for a week, with a little bread and water each day. Two or three weeks after he got out of the sweatbox, he made another escape attempt. When he was recaptured this time, the Germans put him in the hospital basement and tortured him every day. At one point, they twisted his right leg around so his foot was pointing backwards. (He still had a brace on that leg when I interviewed him in 2001.) Ultimately, they upended a bucket on his head and alternated dripping water on the bucket and beating it with sticks.

Years later, *Steve's* doctors sent him to University Hospital in Cleveland to have a CAT scan. *Steve* told me, "They put me on this thing and run me back in this tube. As they're running this thing, it's banging, something's banging—boom, boom, boom, boom, boom." The CAT scan technician had shown *Steve* a ball that he could pull on if he felt so uncomfortable that he needed the technician to stop the scan. He perfectly described the power of a PTSD trigger when he said, "I don't know how long I was in there, but they said when they got me off this conveyor thing, that I had pulled the ball right out of the thing, and I had it in my hand. They had to pry it out of my hand, I had gripped it so tight, and they had to give me shots to knock me out." Later, when the technician and the two nurses asked *Steve* what had happened, "…the only thing I said to them was, 'Please take the bucket off my head. Please take the bucket off of me.' They had no idea. So then they found out that the recurrence was from when they put the bucket on and did that. That's what set it off."

During his eight months of captivity, *Steve* was moved eight times, from his point of capture in eastern Belgium, across the southern part of Germany and finally to Dachau. Though the names of the POW camps changed, the treatment he received was uniformly contemptuous of the Geneva Convention. *Steve* was liberated from Dachau in April 1945, and airlifted to a hospital in France.

Survivor Guilt

As if that weren't enough to deal with, our survivors also suffered from survivor guilt. This emotional reaction to having survived an incident when others did not is officially recognized by the DSM-IV as a symptom of post-traumatic stress order. The accompanying emotional changes may lead to certain anxiety disorders, including phobias. Symptoms of survivor guilt are similar to those of other anxiety disorders, as well as depression. Flashbacks, nightmares, loss of motivation and obsessing about the event are common. Recovering from survivor guilt can be accomplished on your own or with the help of supportive friends, family, or professional therapists.

During my years as a psychotherapist, I counseled many clients dealing with survivor guilt. While I often dealt with the aftermath of loss of a beloved family member or partner, my most traumatized clients were parents who had lost children.[26] These parents and each of our survivors shared a common struggle with the question of "Why?" Why did I survive and my friend did not?" "Why did I survive and the rest of my family did not?" "Why did I survive and so many from my unit did not?" The feelings associated with the resulting survivor guilt are a heavy weight to bear, even as they defy rational explanation. Thaddeus

Stabholz puts it this way: "It was very difficult to survive. You think you are happy forever when released, but in the beginning you have more guilt than happiness."

Judith Altmann was born in Czechoslovakia in 1925, one of six children in her family. She was 14 years old when Germany invaded Poland in 1939 and began dividing the Jewish people between who could work and who would be sent to death.[27] Prior to that, she said, "It was very democratic, like in the U.S. There was no discrimination." After Hitler occupied the country, men were drafted into labor camps and never seen again. Children were removed from school. All Jewish businesses were confiscated, including her father's prosperous general store where, Judith said, "one could buy everything from a needle to a horse." The store continued to operate but all proceeds were diverted to the government.

As in other occupied countries, Jews were forced into ghettos and had to wear two Stars of David, one on the arm and one on the back. In 1944, Judy was arrested and sent to Auschwitz, then on to the Essen and Gelsenkirchen labor camps. She remained there until March 1945, when she was part of the Death March to Bergen Belsen where she was liberated by British forces that May.[28] Her intense feelings associated with survivor guilt had not yet lost their power when I interviewed her in 2003. She said, "Ask survivors, 'Do you remember the guilt?' Because we do. We all felt we were selected. 'Why? Why not my sister? Why not my mother? Why did my mother and my sister die?' And you live with that, and you say to yourself, 'Why me?' And we all have it. You couldn't answer it in your mind. You don't ask it. Just being in the wrong place at the wrong time but not being picked by Mengele."

Even though the guilt is still there for Joe Diamond, he found a way to turn the Why?" into something productive: "Sometimes you feel guilty that you are alive when some of the people are gone. Most people that got to Auschwitz died within a short time. A lot of religious people died immediately, so their answer to that is, 'God loved them so much he wanted them first.' Here I wasn't particularly religious and I'm alive. My answer to that is, 'I'm around to tell the story. God wants me to tell the story.'"

Finding the Strength to Share the Story

After liberation, our survivors had to face the monumental task of re-integrating themselves into society. Even if they had support from family, friends and/or survivor organizations, trying to adapt to the relative comfort and ease of life back at home was stressful. For those who were alone, creating "home" in unfamiliar surroundings was yet another kind of trauma. Sharing their experiences certainly would have helped ease their transitions, but hardly any of them could do that at the time. The few who tried found no one who could grasp the depth of what they had been through; many of them waited twenty or thirty or forty years to start sharing their stories. Once they did, though, they quickly learned that hearing stories of the Holocaust directly from someone who was there made an indelible impression on students of every age. The satisfaction they felt at keeping that history alive represents the essence of circular support.

Meanwhile, every survivor had a huge and difficult transition to manage. Most came out of prison with PTSD, and had to come to terms with its life-long effects. The most recently freed of the survivors you've met in this book, Ahmed Kathrada, returned to his own home 20 years ago. The Vietnam survivors have been home almost 40 years, the Korea survivors more than 50 years and the World War II survivors more than 60 years. Regardless of the length of time between *then* and *now*, many survivors still find it difficult to talk about their experiences, except with a fellow survivor. Alex Ehrmann emigrated to the U.S. after World War II. He lived in Montreal, then New York, before settling in Detroit in 1960. He buried the memories of the Holocaust and found solace only in his work. As he told me, "I forgot. I couldn't deal with it at all. I couldn't get myself to talk with others, but once I started talking about it, it was very therapeutic for me. I couldn't get myself to cry after the war, and usually when I got into a conversation with a non-survivor, a few minutes would go by and I'd say to myself, 'What are you talking about? These people don't understand you anyway.' And I stopped talking about it. It wasn't until 1960 or so that I almost broke down and cried…."

A few years later, an organization called the Children of Survivors invited Alex to speak to them and share his feelings. Standing in front of that group, surrounded by other survivors, he found his voice. "In Washington, all of the survivors being together, I relived concentration camp—the hustling and jostling and pushing and shoving, the same way as it was in the concentration camp. When I went to share my feelings, it just busted out of me and I said, 'I survived!' That's all I said. Realizing that Hitler is dead and I'm alive, that feeling has never left me. It was absolutely empowering, the more I spoke about it." Alex became a popular speaker with all kinds of organizations, and regularly spoke to groups at the Holocaust Memorial Center in Detroit. "I never stopped to think about it being a courageous thing to do. I just know it's rewarding for me and that prompts me more every occasion. I'm glad I do this."

Joe Diamond also sees the big picture, especially when he is speaking with students: "We're not doing this for ourselves. Our people are gone. We are doing this for future generations. Jewish people today! It can happen, believe me. All you have to do is change the government, change dictatorial people, and people are gonna follow when conditions are bad in the country. That's why we are out speaking in schools. We have to respect each other."

When I interviewed Judith Altmann, she was most excited to tell me about how she had been sharing her story, and the stories of women she met in the concentration camps, with school children. Judith said, "I told them about a mother, a young mother that was in her early twenties. She had three children. She was chosen to go to work, to live, and her children went with her mother, their grandmother, to the gas chamber. I think we were still in Auschwitz when she composed a beautiful song, and the words of the song were, 'There are no more Sarahs, Joes and Peters to sing and to play.' Many people wrote songs and poems. I

have a whole book of poems written by the children in Theresienstadt, called, 'We are Children Just the Same.'"

Each time she visits a school, Judith has a special point she
emphasizes. "Do not carry hate because hate destroys you, not
the hated one. The person that you hate doesn't know you're
hating him. But inside, you are killing yourself with hate. And
if you can overcome that, then you're all right." Just before our
interview, Judith had spoken to a large group of children during
a one-day visit to a private school. I could easily see how touched
she was by their response, when she said, "They sent me beautiful
thank-you letters and they sent me the most magnificent scroll."
When she unfurled it to show me, it stretched all the way across
her living room. Every student from the classes to whom she had
generously and courageously told her story had signed the scroll.
It was covered with messages of thanks and caring. One of the
notes said, "I admire you and how you were able to deal with all
those people dying around you. I would not have been able to
survive such things, but you could, even when you were a teenager. Thank you for telling your story." That scroll is one of Judith's
most prized possessions.

Steve also coped with the memories of his prison-camp experiences by sharing his story with school children across Ohio.
These first-hand reports have made World War II history come
vividly alive for the students, who are uniformly spellbound by
his edited version of the realities of war. He admits to being really
nervous before his very first session with students. As he was
walking up to the building, he overheard a kid bragging about
having just turned sixteen years old and going to get his driver's
license. A light-bulb went on in *Steve's* mind and he knew exactly
what he wanted to say.

After ascertaining that some seventeen-year-olds were in the
classroom, *Steve* told them what he had been doing at seventeen:
"When I was seventeen years old I enlisted in the Army. I was
not drafted. I enlisted. My parents didn't want me to go, but I
said, 'I'll go even if you don't want me to.' You guys know how you
do it. Your mom and dad tells you, 'Don't speed going down the

road.' Well, you're going to speed anyway. You get in the car and go speed." *Steve* thought he was in for the greatest adventure of his life, going overseas to all these countries he never dreamed of seeing. He continued, "But there's one thing that I never thought about, that would be getting captured. I said, 'So you just think about it the next that you get behind the wheel of an automobile and you go 50 mile an hour down a 35 mile an hour zone. If a policeman picks you up, he don't take you to jail. He isn't going to take your car. Maybe he'll lock you up for the next ten months, and you won't see your mother and father, you won't get to take a bath, you ain't going to get nothing. Now, that's the start of being a prisoner of war.' You ought to seen the expression on these kids."

Emotional support, rare enough among the prisoners in the camps, could be equally rare after liberation. In the years after the war, Adrienne Krausz came home from the concentration camp, got married within six months and had a daughter during the first year of her marriage. But she ran into a wall of incomprehension whenever she tried to tell someone about what she had been through: "They said to us after the war, 'Well, you went just like sheeps.' I would give it to them! 'How can you say that, when you weigh 60 or 70 pounds and you see a soldier with ammunition, with rifles, with German Shepherds around? How can you fight against them? You have to obey so you hope maybe you will survive.'"

When her daughter turned fifteen, Adrienne and she had their first conversation about the Holocaust. Adrienne said, "I never told her about anything. I was so tight-mouthed, I couldn't talk to anybody about it. Then my daughter said to me, 'Mother, you know you never told me anything about your parents, how you were as a kid. What happened?' And then I started to talk, because she asked me." As more and more people heard Adrienne tell her story, invitations to speak began to arrive. She continued, "They started to ask me to talk to children in school, and that's how I came to open up. Now I can talk freely about it, without even crying when I'm talking. At the beginning I was crying always, I couldn't finish my sentences. It's very difficult to talk, because you talk to people who don't know what it means to be…. I mean it's an inhuman existence." Through all these presentations, Adrienne came to believe that there was still a missing piece of her story, something else she needed her daughter to understand. "I'm taking my daughter and my granddaughter there, because I don't know how long I'm going to live. I want them to see it because it's different to read it in books and different to hear it. I want them to see the camps, to see for themselves what it was, because I think it's important that they have this legacy. They should know what happened."

Finding someone willing to listen and able to understand, was equally difficult for *Ann*. In 1939, *Ann* was 17 years old, living a comfortable life in Lodz, Poland with her parents, brother and sister. The family had a successful business making suits, coats and school uniforms. *Ann* wanted to be an accountant, and she loved ice skating and collecting stamps, butterflies and autographs of famous movie stars. Everything changed in April 1940, when the Nazis moved 164,000 Jews into a rundown section of the city. *Ann's* family was forced to abandon their home and their business to take up residence in a one-room "apartment" in the Lodz ghetto. Her mother was allowed to stay "at home" in the ghetto while the rest of the family was assigned to work: her brother at city hall, her sister and father at a textile factory. *Ann* was sent to a shoe factory, where she used big needles and her bare hands to make straw overshoes to insulate the boots of German soldiers fighting on the Russian front. She told me, "Next to me at the factory sat two young girls too sick and weak to work. I knew they would never be able to produce their daily quota of four boots each day and they would surely lose their job. I was a fast worker and could produce as many as twelve boots a day. I divided my work in three so that each of the girls would have their daily quota and not be taken away as unproductive workers. In this way I was able to keep those girls alive for four years until the ghetto was liquidated."

In 1944, after the liquidation, *Ann's* family was transported to Auschwitz in cattle cars. Her father had been one of 800 men selected to stay behind and clean up the ghetto, but he refused to be separated from his family. It was a tragic "which cliff?" decision. All 800 men survived until liberation, but *Ann's* father and brother were murdered in the gas chamber shortly after they arrived in Auschwitz. *Ann* and her sister were taken to a different gas chamber, but sheer luck was on their side: the chamber was not functioning and they were saved. The sisters spent ten days in Auschwitz and then were transported to Bergen Belsen. After six more weeks, they were shipped to Salzwedel, Germany to work in an ammunition factory making bullets (and, as you already read, sabotaging them) for the German war effort. Shortly before liberation, the German officials overseeing the camp were given orders to electrocute the girls working at the factory so there would be no witnesses. They refused to carry out their orders. Meanwhile, the defective bullets came back from the front line, but American soldiers liberated the labor camp before the Germans could discover who was responsible (Paull, 1998).

Once she had married and settled in Rochester, New York, people often asked *Ann* about what she had been through. As she tried to tell them how it had been, she quickly discovered that the experiential gap between her and her American friends was unbridgeable. The trauma of not having anybody understand what she had been through compounded the trauma of the original experience. She told me, "Nobody wanted to know. They say, 'How are you?' and even I know you have to say, 'Fine, thank you.' They said, 'Forget about what was. You in a new country. Learn the language. You have a family now, a little baby and a husband. Forget about what was.' I didn't say nothing back to them, but I felt…if they would kill *your* family…not only I lost my father, mine brother, my mother, I lost all my uncles and aunts and cousins. It's a big family to lose." After learning the tough lesson that there was no emotional support to be found in her "new country," *Ann* kept quiet for 40 years. "Forty years, we didn't speak about nothing. Everything we hold in our self because nobody wanted to listen."

In 1987, an Auschwitz exhibit of large photographic posters with explanatory captions was brought to Rochester by the local Jewish Federation and the Mennonite Central Committee. The two groups had called on area survivors to come and help augment the facts in the poster captions with their first-hand accounts. *Ann* went, but not for that reason. "We went for another reason—to see maybe on the posters, we gonna find somebody from the family. This was our goal, really, to go. We didn't want to speak at all, just to go, see and goodbye. Not to tell nobody. Nobody wants to listen."

As she stood there, she found herself responding instinctively to the first sympathetic listener she had ever encountered, someone who had come with a group of friends to see the exhibit. *Ann* said, "I'm staying by a poster how we slept in the bunk beds, and somebody, a lady behind me, said to the few people, 'Must have been terrible!' because they show the way we slept. I turn around. This was first time I opened my mouth after 40 years, and I said, 'Yes, it was terrible. I was there.' And they all said, 'Please, please tell me the story what really happened.' So I started to speak, but was tough on me, was very tough on me. My face was wet from tears. When I went home, I'm sitting down and thinking, 'I am not brave. Why all of a sudden I'm speaking?' So, I start to go back, how I survived, how many times I was just ready to be killed, and through miracles I survived. I said, 'Why shouldn't I tell the story? I never gave up in my life and all through the war. Let people know so that my loved ones didn't die in vain.' And that the way I start to speak."

Once she had begun to talk about her experiences, *Ann* says she completely switched the focus of her life to speaking with students. Their responses leave no doubt that what she is doing is important: "The kids always say in letters, 'Please don't stop, don't stop speaking. Educate the kids, let them really know.' Because they feel, they write to me. Books, movies, notes can't make the impact. But when they see a survivor with their emotions, with the details what I'm telling them, it's unbearable. You can't see it, you can't write, because what we saw and I explain to the kids, they feel like they owe it to me. They feel the hurt, what I went through."

Ann is skilled at making the connection between her Holocaust memories and the big issues kids have to face today: "Respect is the most important, respect for the next person, respect for the teacher because the teacher is our future. Respect for each other's religion, color or creed. We are all God's children. I said, 'Why you making groups in school? You think you better than the other? Why stay by when you see your friend is picked on? Don't let it happen.' It's very important. And they cry. So, to make them smile, I said, 'As long as God gives me the marbles in my head and I'll be healthy, I will speak. I will never stop if people want to listen because people have to know. And this is my goal in life.'"

Thaddeus Stabholz feels deeply his obligation to be a witness to history. He said, "Some survivors didn't talk at all for many years, they tried to forget about it. But I have a different idea. I was a witness wherever it happened and I wanted to talking to as many people as I could. Just to teach, whatever I thought it was worth. To different groups, students, colleges, to teachers…to church groups, whenever I could. So in years I have quite a few." Mirroring Adrienne's reluctance to share the most difficult details of her history with her daughter, Thaddeus also found it easier to tell others what happened than to tell his own daughter. But she ended up reaching him in a way no one else could have. He told me, "When my daughter, Peggy, was young, when I was younger, once during the night she said, 'Daddy, what is that number?' (pointing to the number tattooed on his arm). I said, 'Oh, honey, it's a telephone number, a very important telephone number I have to remember.'

But when she was sixteen, I took her to Poland, I took her to Auschwitz and to Treblinka. Before we went to Auschwitz it was 1965 or 1966. It was a small museum, it was not much, it was a lot of glasses, a lot of big glass [display cases], like half of a wall. In photographs there were two prisoners, dead prisoners, lying on the ground, their arms were somehow crossed. On one arm she saw the number 126603; on the other one was 126605. I was 604. And I was taking the photographs and I saw her crying. I didn't know what…I took a picture of her crying. She knew what the number means."

Notes

24. www.ncbi.nlm.nih.gov/pubmed
25. www.mayoclinic.com/health/post-traumatic-stress-disorder
26. I often recommended an organization called Compassionate Friends (www.compassionatefriends.org) that has chapters all over the country to offer grief support after the loss of a child at any age from any cause.
27. www.newcanaan.patch.com, February 18, 2011; www.farmington.patch.com, February 2011.
28. Holocaust & Human Right Education Center

Chapter Eight

SHRINK THINKING:
A VIEW FROM THE THERAPIST'S CHAIR

I cannot imagine my life without this body of work, without having gotten to know these survivors, or without having had my own Gestalt moment of closure as my personal and professional lives came together. On the personal side, in the mid-1960s, my energy levels were very low and I was having to prop myself up with a couple of pillows at night to facilitate my breathing and sleep comfortably. I kept thinking I had the flu, but it wasn't getting better and, in some ways, it was getting worse. When I finally consulted my family doctor about the symptoms, he said, "There's a thing called myasthenia gravis" and sent me to a specialist. The subsequent testing confirmed my doctor's instincts and formalized the diagnosis. Myasthenia gravis is a neuromuscular, autoimmune disorder, the exact cause of which is unknown. Symptoms are all related to weaknesses of the voluntary or skeletal muscles, e.g., breathing difficulty, double vision and general fatigue. These worsen with over-activity and improve with rest. The disorder is often managed well, in fact, with a combination of medication and adequate rest.

Following that pattern, I have had long periods of remission over the last 40 years. During those times, I don't even think about the myasthenia and have no hesitation to travel or take on any of those strenuous sports I love: cross-country and downhill skiing, snorkeling and scuba diving, and long walks with my dogs. But I have learned that on any given morning, I could wake up to an episode, usually characterized by shortness of breath and fatigue. Those symptoms give me no choice but to adjust my activities to include lots of rest. Learning to adapt to my circumstances on a daily basis continues to be vital to my health. For my interviewees, that same adaptive skill was vital to their very survival.

On the professional side, given my background as a psychologist/psychotherapist, it was inevitable that I would look at the work of producing this book as an extension of my career. If I were still seeing clients, they would benefit from what I have learned through the interviews and the writing process. When I consider why my interviews went so well, I am convinced that my own physical appearance was an asset. It is fair to say that women generally are perceived as less threatening than men. White-haired grannies like me, especially those of us under five feet tall, are less threatening than just about anyone else. My demeanor, honed through my active psychotherapy years, wordlessly encouraged trust and enabled open conversation.

Other psychotherapy skills also enhanced each interview. For example, the formation of my questions reflected patterns common to client sessions over the years. I asked the survivors a mix of yes/no questions and open-ended questions. In my client sessions, I never had a set list of questions, but formulated them on the fly in response to what the client was working on at the time. Having a set list of questions for the survivors didn't mean that I never ad libbed, sometimes changing the course of the conversations as needed to elicit more in-depth information. The answers to those questions were also filtered through my well-developed "shrink-eye."

Years of counseling had honed my instincts to simultaneously process words, their underlying feelings and body language to gain not just information, but also a unique impression of viewpoint and attitude. I was equipped to notice second-by-second feedback about each interviewee's emotional state during our conversation. Important non-verbal clues included changes in breathing, in eye contact (e.g., staring at the ceiling or the floor or anywhere but at me), in the sound of the voice, and in an increasing physical restlessness—all visible indicators of normal inner processing of experiences. All these clues allowed me to do two things during the course of any given session or interview. First, I knew when to say nothing and simply wait quietly for the client/survivor to process feelings raised by what had just been said. The second was to better understand the person with whom I was speaking—a vital tool in maintaining the intentionally created safe environment that evoked such open sharing. In short, I was using my personal and professional history to notice how the survivors managed to cope, before and after their release, without textbooks, stress-management classes, sessions with a pastor or counselor, or medications from the family doctor. They just figured it out.

A surprising development snuck up on me over the course of all the interviews. My lifelong fascination with the way people reflect on their life experiences fueled my enthusiasm for a long and successful career. Since I was a trained listener/responder, attentive and respectful as I traveled with my clients to new understandings of their issues, I was confident that those well-practiced skills would carry over easily into the interview process. Early on, however, I encountered a totally unexpected joy: No Therapy Required! I hadn't fully realized how it would feel to have these intimate conversations free of any obligation for me to interpret or evaluate what I heard. No confidential files. No insurance paperwork to complete. No letters to family doctors. I still needed consent and release forms, of course, but only in the context of being able to share what I heard and learned—something I had never been able to do in my work.

No Neutral Listeners

In a direct contrast to my work as a therapist, a unique quality of these prison environments was that there were no neutral listeners. In my interactions with clients, I played a complementary role, offering active listening, feedback, and emotional support. Successive sessions in my journey with each client built a bridge of trust between us, allowing me to help the client move from anxiety, stress or depression to a level of understanding, then coping, with the issues at hand. In all the prison settings, on the other hand, everyone with whom a survivor might exchange a few words was also emotionally stressed, physically exhausted and starving. No one could assume the objective role of a counselor. As a result, the typical dialogue of interpersonal support was sometimes supplanted by what I call "monologues in the company of others." Each would voice his or her own concerns, and the other would do the same.

Murray Ebner was born in 1928 in Wisnicz, Poland, the son of a farm-products wholesaler. He was 12 years old when his family hid in the woods near their town after the Germans invaded Poland in 1939. Once a law had been passed that anyone not in the Warsaw Ghetto would be shot, the family came out of hiding and sought what they thought would be refuge in the Ghetto. Young Murray, who was now 13, was immediately separated from his family and never saw his parents again. One day he was told to get on a truck with all the other children. When they arrived at a cemetery, all the children were told to jump off the truck and line up behind some men at a table. Small children faced certain death, but the guard assigning children to one group or the other thought Murray looked strong enough to work and said, "I mark you down as 16 years." Murray then learned that those under 16 and over 50 were all shot. Ultimately, Murray would be taken from the Warsaw Ghetto to Birkenau and subjected to four years of hard labor in a cemetery in Auschwitz, then forced to march for miles to Trzebinia, then back to Auschwitz.[29]

Murray remembers that, in some circumstances, the situation was so terrible there was no energy, no will, to provide or even to receive interpersonal support. He said, "I was able to talk to the guys in my barracks, but our conversation was never really conversation. Just came to lie down, lay down in our bed. There was no conversation. In the army, you know, we're buddies. There was a bunk over here and there's a bunk over there. We sit down. We talked about different things. Over there, in the concentration camp, there was no such thing. No such thing. No camaraderie. But talking with others helped take away the loneliness. And I know I was sad. And everybody around me was sad. Each one was thinking about their own families. We did not try to make friends. There was no laughter down there. We knew it was serious business and every day we just went to work, came back, say, 'I'm tired. I got to lay down.' And that's all. The next day, the same. There was no friendship because we didn't know what to expect the next day."

Remember the Gestalt Cycle of Experience you read about in the Introduction? Murray's story is a clear illustration of that cycle, as is this next story about Bob Shumaker. Bob had had some experience in construction and building houses earlier in his life, before his military service landed him in a North Vietnamese POW camp. With lots of time on his hands, he began to daydream about a house he would like to build when he got back home. That dream became his intrapersonal support, his go-to place to divert his mind from his present circumstances. The more he thought about that house, the more determined he was to draw out the plan. The project fascinated him so much that after he had drawn the plans, he began to figure out how much lumber he would need, how many windows and doors there should be, and even how many nails it would take to put the whole house together. In a personal postscript to this story, I interviewed Bob at his home in Virginia, in the house he had planned in such meticulous detail in his North Vietnam prison cell.

The shared history of my 46 interviewees is not recorded anywhere else except in this book. I began this project with the goal of gathering first-hand information about how people in life-threatening situations dealt with stress. That initial step led to an in-depth study of prison-camp survivors and the coping skills that helped them. Until now, the resulting interviews have been a private joy in my own life. Even though my myasthenia gravis has progressed to the point where reading even my own book is problematic, my joy at sharing the survivors' stories with you is undiminished.

Over the course of this brief volume, you have encountered both hell and hope. My own hope for you is that you have been moved to feel a connection with at least one of these awe-inspiring survivors. If so, you are now in a position to be, in Jacob Hennenberg's words, a "witness for the witness." I ask you to take that role to heart and share that survivor's story. In doing so, you will help me realize my original goal of honoring these men and women and passing their stories into the hands, hearts and minds of the next generations.

Notes

29. The New Standard, a publication of Jewish Family Services, Columbus, Ohio; special supplement for Yom Hashoah 5765, 60 Years After the Holocaust.

THE SURVIVORS

Holocaust Survivors

Judith Altmann .. .. Interviewed June 16, 2003, Stamford, CT

Henry Blumenfeld .. .. Interviewed October 2, 2001, Rochester, NY

Joe Diamond.. .. .. Interviewed July 25, 2002, Buffalo, NY

Murray Ebner .. .. Interviewed May 1, 2002, Columbus, OH

Alex Ehrmann . .. . Interviewed May 23, 2001, Detroit, MI

Ginny . .. . Interviewed June 21, 2001. (Pseudonym used at the request of the interviewee.)

Henry Greenbaum .. .. Interviewed June 21, 2002, Washington, DC

Jack Gun. .. .. Interviewed May 25, 2001, Bloomfield, MI

Marian Haszlakiewicz . .. .. . Interviewed November 4, 2003, Sarasota, FL

Jacob Hennenberg .. .. Interviewed January 20, 2003, Beachwood, OH

Adrienne Krausz .. .. Interviewed June 13, 2003, Westport, CT

Harry & Emmy Loeb .. .. Interviewed October 31, 2003, Port Charlotte, FL

Ben Lohman .. .. Interviewed December 1, 2003, Fairway, KS

Sonia & Max Mentelmacher.. Interviewed October 29, 2001, Rochester, NY

Ann .. .. Interviewed October 31, 2001. (Pseudonym used at the request of the interviewee.)

Thaddeus Stabholz.. .. .. Interviewed October 2, 2001, Canton, OH

Hans. .. .. Interviewed October 29, 1996. (Pseudonym used at the request of the interviewee.)

Vic (deceased) .. .. Interviewed his sister. (Pseudonym used at the request of the interviewee.)

Martin Weiss.. .. .. Interviewed June 19, 2002, Bethesda, MD

Stanley Wiczyk .. .. Interviewed July 25, 2003, Erie, PA

Al. .. .. Interviewed, by phone, April 7, 2005, Portland, OR (Pseudonym used at the request of the interviewee.)

Ex-Prisoners of War

Albert Allen. U.S. Army – World War II, Pacific Theatre; Tank Battalion; held for five years. Interviewed September 3, 2002, Mansfield, OH

Bill. U.S. Army – Vietnam; S/Sgt.. (Pseudonym used at the request of the interviewee.)

Lawrence J. "Doc" Bott. U.S. Army – World War II, Germany; Combat Medic, Infantry, I Co., 3rd Battalion, 30th Regiment; held for 4-1/2 months. Interviewed September 17, 2002, Columbus, OH

Curtis Brooks. World War II, Pacific Theatre, Philippines; held in Japanese Internment Camp for 37 months. Interviewed January 22, 2002, Alexandria, VA

Charles Brutza. U.S. Army, World War II, Germany; Infantry/Medic, 45th Division; held for less than one month. Interviewed January 23, 2002, Washington, DC

Carl Cossin. U.S. Army, World War II, European Theatre, Paratrooper, 10th Mountain Infantry Division. U.S. Army, World War II, Pacific Theatre. U.S. Army, Korea, 24th Division; held for three years. Interviewed September 26, 2002, Columbus, OH

Neal Harrington. U.S. Army, World War II, Pacific Theatre; held for 3-1/2 years). Interviewed January 19, 2002, Location Unknown.

Patrick Hart. World War II, Pacific Theatre, Philippines; held in Japanese Internment Camp for 37 months. Interviewed October 20, 2004, Granville, OH

Will. U.S. Army Air Forces, World War II, Germany; Navigator; held for two years. (Pseudonym used at the request of the interviewee.)

Harry. U.S. Air Force, World War II, Germany; Colonel, Lead Bombadier; held for an unknown length of time. (Pseudonym used at the request of the interviewee.)

Dick Mann. U.S. Naval Reserve, World War II, Pacific Theatre; LT. [jg], Pilot, Bombing Squadron 83; held for six weeks. Interviewed June 4, 2001, Granville, OH

Hank. U.S. Army Air Force, World War II, Germany; held for approximately one year. (Pseudonym used at the request of the interviewee.)

Corwin "Bud" Morey. U.S. Marine Corps, World War II, Pacific Theater; held for 40 months. Interviewed April 3, 2004, Columbus, OH

Charles Mott. U.S. Navy Air Corps, World War II, Japan; held for 3-1/2 years. Interviewed January 12, 2002, Vienna, VA

Bob Phillips. U.S. Army, World War II, Pacific Theatre; Chaplain; held for an unknown length of time. Interviewed November 29, 2002, Maitland, FL

Bob Shumaker. U.S. Navy, Vietnam; LT. CMDR, Fighter Squadron 154; held for eight years. Interviewed January 17, 2002, Fairfax Station, VA

Steve. U.S. Army, World War II, Germany; Infantry, 3rd/5th/99th Divisions; held for eight months. (Pseudonym used at the request of the interviewee.)

Michael Stroff. U.S. Army Air Corps OR U.S. Navy??, World War II, Germany; held for 18 months. Interviewed June 9, 2002, McLean, VA

Alfred Tibor. Hungarian Army, World War II; held for five years by the Russians in Siberia. Interviewed July 2, 2001, Columbus, OH

Bob. U.S. Army, World War II, Germany; held for 4-1/2 months. (Pseudonym used at the request of the interviewee.)

Claude Watkins. U.S. Army Air Forces, World War II, Germany; S/Sgt waistgunner/armorer, 331st Squadron, 94th Bomber Group, Eighth Air Force; held for 18 months). Interviewed June 23, 2002, Washington, DC

Former Political Prisoners

James. Cold War, East Germany; held for seven months. (Pseudonym used at the request of the interviewee.)

Ahmed Kathrada. Political dissident/activist, Republic of South Africa; held for 26+ years. Interviewed August 3, 2000, Chautauqua, NY

Peng Ming-Min. Political dissident/activist, Taiwan; repeatedly arrested and held until his eventual escape. Interviewed October 25, 1992, Los Angeles, CA

REFERENCES

American Psychiatric Association. (1994). Diagnotics and statistical manual of mental disorders: DSM-IV. (1994). Washington, DC: Author.

Anderson, M. (2002). My lord, what a morning. Chicago: University of Illinois Press. (Original work published 1956.)

Applebaum, B. & Marchant, P. (2003). Angie's Story. Rochester, NY: Jewish Federation of Rochester.

Beck, A. T. (1976). Cognitive therapy and the emotional disorders. New York: International Universities Press.

Berscheid, E. (2003). The human's greatest strength: Other humans. In L. Aspinwall & U. Staudinger (Eds.), A psychology of human strengths: Fundamental questions and future directions for a positive psychology (pp. 37-47). Washington, DC: American Psychological Association.

Breuer, W. B. (2002). The great raid: rescuing the doomed ghosts of Bataan and Corregidor. New York: Hyperion Press. (Originally published in hardcover by John Wiley & Sons, Inc.)

Brickhill, P. (1950). The great escape. New York: W. W. Norton & Company, Inc.

Gilbert, M. (2007). Kristallnacht: Prelude to destruction. New York: HarperCollins Publishers.

Helmstetter, S. (1991). What to say when you talk to your self. Wellborough: Thorsons.

Hennenberg, J. (date unknown). Tell us papa what happened there. Self-published.

Hubbell, J.C. (1976). P.O.W.: A definitive history of the American prisoner-of-war experience in Vietnam, 1964-1973. Reader's Digest Press, New York. Pp 33, 36, 37-38

Kathrada, A. (2000). Letters from Robben Island: A selection of Ahmed Kathrada's prison correspondence, 1964-1989. East Lansing, MI: Michigan State University Press.

Milgram, S. (1983). Obedience to authority: An experimental view. New York: HarperCollins Publishers.

Nevis, E. D. (1987). Organizational consulting: A Gestalt approach. Cleveland, OH: Gestalt Institute of Cleveland Press.

Paull, A.S. (1998). I call myself a miracle kid: Angie's story. Rochester, NY: Center for Holocaust Awareness and Information of the Jewish Community Federation.

Perls, F. S., Hefferline, R. & Goodwin, P. (1994). Gestalt therapy: Excitement and growth in the human personality. Cleveland, OH: Gestalt Journal Press Edition.

Selye, H. (1976). The stress of life. (2nd ed.). New York: McGraw-Hill Book Co.

Steffen, L. (2003). The demonic turn: The power of religion to inspire or restrain violence. New York: Pilgrim Press.

RELATED READINGS & RESOURCES

Interviewee Autobiographies/Biographies

Bergen, B. (2012). A tiger on the River Kwai: AVG flying tiger pilot Charles D. Mott, an interview (Flying Tigers). Banana Tree Press.

Cossin, C. (2001). I soldiered with America's elite 10th Mountain Division of W.W.II. AuthorHouse.

Cossin, C. (2001). Raw Guts. 1st Books Library.

Ebner, M. (2010). Chosen for reasons unknown: A survivor's journey. AtlasBooks/Lucky Charm Publishing.

Feldman, G. (2008). Saved by the spirit of Lafayette. Northville, MI: Nelson Publishing & Marketing.

Greenspan, H. (1998). Listening to Holocaust survivors. In R. Josselson, A. Lieblich & D. McAdams, Up close and personal: The teaching and learning of narrative research (pp 101-111). Washington, DC: American Psychological Association.

Haszlakiewicz, Z. (1996). Madness of the twentieth century: A testimony. Sarasota, FL: Z. M. Haszlakiewicz.

Ming-min, P. (2nd ed.). (1994). A taste of freedom: Memoirs of a Formosan independence leader. Taiwan Publishing Company.

Stabholz, T. (1990). Seven hells. Ann Arbor: Holocaust Library/University of Michigan. (Originally printed in a displaced persons camp in Stuttgart, West Germany shortly after liberation.)

Tibor, A. (2012). Celebration of life: The Tibor story as told to Judy Perry Kurimai. Studio T, Inc.

Wiener, A. (2007). From a name to a number: A Holocaust survivor's autobiography. AuthorHouse.

Psychology

Aldwin, C. (1994). Stress, coping and development. New York: The Guilford Press.

Antonovsky, A. (1979). Health, stress and coping. San Francisco: Jossey-Bass Publishing.

Bandura, A. (1977). Self-efficacy: Toward a unifying theory of behavioral c"Hans"ge. Psychological Review, 84, 191-215.

Benezra, E. (1996). Personality factors of individuals who survive traumatic experiences without professional help. International Journal of Stress Management, 3, 147-153.

Berger, L. (1988). The longterm psychological consequences of the Holocaust on the survivors and their offspring. In R. L. Braham (Ed.), The psychological perspectives of the Holocaust and its aftermath (pp.72-215). New York: The Institute for Holocaust Studies, the Graduate School and University Center, City University of New York.

Bowlby, J. (1973). Self-reliance and the conditions that promote it. In R. Gosling (Ed.), Support, innovation and autonomy. London: Tavistock Publishers, Ltd.

Braiker, H. (1989, December). The power of self-talk. Psychology Today, 23-27.

Branham, R. (Ed.). (1988). The psychological perspectives of the Holocaust and its aftermath. In Social Science Monographs. Ann Arbor: The University of Michigan Press.

Calhoun, L. & Tedeschi, R. (1999). Facilitating posttraumatic growth. Mahwah, NJ: Lawrence Erlbaum Associates.

Cohler, B. (1987). Adversity, resilience and the study of lives. In E. Anthony & B. Cohler (Eds.), The invulnerable child (363-424). New York: The Guilford Press.

Denzin, N. & Lincoln, Y. (Eds.). (2000). Handbook of qualitative research. (2nd ed.). Thousand Oaks, CA: Sage Publications, Inc.

Eitinger, L. & Major, E. (1993). Stress of the holocaust. In L. Goldberger & S. Breznitz (Eds.), Handbook of stress: Theoretical and clinical aspects. (2nd ed.). New York: The Free Press.

Figley, C.R. (1978). Stress disorders among Vietnam veterans: Theory, research and treatment. (Routledge Psychosocial Stress Series). New York: Brunner/Mazel.

Flannery, R. B., Jr. (1996). Post-traumatic stress disorder: The victim's guide to healing and recovery. New York: Crossroad Publishing Company.

Gladwell, M. (2007). Blink: The power of thinking without thinking. New York: Little, Brown and Company.

Herman, J. L. (1992). Trauma and recovery. New York: Basic Books.

Higgins, G. O. (1994). Resilient adults: Overcoming a cruel past. San Francisco: Jossey Bass Publishing.

Hofball, S. & Vaux, A. (1993). Social support: resources and context. In L. Goldberger & S. Breznitz, Handbook of stress: Theoretical and clinical aspects. (2nd ed.). (685-705). New York: The Free Press.

Horowitz, M. (1982). Stress response syndromes. New York: Jason Aronson, Inc.

Isen, A. (2003). Positive affect as a source of human strength. In L. Aspinwall & U. Staudinger, A psychology of human strengths: Fundamental question and future directions for a positive psychology. Washington, DC: American Psychological Association.

Maddi, S. (2002). The story of hardiness: Twenty years of theorizing, research and practice. Consulting Psychology Journal, 54, 173-185.

Rosenbaum, M. (Ed.) (1990). Learned resourcefulness: On coping skills, self-control and adaptive behavior. New York: Springer Publishing Company.

Schiraldi, G. (2009). The post-traumatic stress disorder scourcebook: A guide to healing, recovery and growth (2nd ed.). New York: McGraw-Hill.

Seligman, M. (1991). Learned optimism: How to change your mind and your life. New York: Alfred A. Knopf.

Seligman, E. P. & Csikszentmihalyi, M. (2000). Positive psychology: An introduction. American Psychologist, 55, (1), 5-14.

Shapiro, F. (2001). Eye movement desensitization and reprocessing (EMDR): Basic principles, protocols, and procedures (2nd ed.). New York: The Guilford Press.

Tedeschi, R., Park, C. & Calhoun, L. (1998). Posttraumatic growth: positive changes in the aftermath of crisis. Mahwah, NJ: Lawrence Erlbaum Associates.

Vaillant, G. (2000). Adaptive mental mechanisms: Their role in a positive psychology. American Psychologist, 55, (1) 89-98.

Van der Kolk, B., McFarlane, A. & Weisaeth, L. (Eds.). (1996). Traumatic stress: The effects of overwhelming experience on mind, body, and society. New York: The Guilford Press.

Weintraub, S. (2002). Silent Night: The story of the World War I Christmas truce. New York: Penguin-Putnam, Inc.

Weisberg, R. (2006). Creativity: Understanding innovation in problem solving, science, invention, and the arts. Hoboken, NJ: John Wiley & Sons.

Whiteman, D. (1993). Holocaust survivors and escapees—their strengths. Psychotherapy: Theory, research, practice, training, 30, 443-451.

Winick, M. (Ed.) (1979). Hunger disease: Studies by the Jewish physicians in the Warsaw Ghetto. New York: Wiley & Sons.

Young-Eisendrath, P. (1996). The resilient spirit: Transforming suffering into insight and renewal. New York: Addison-Wesley Publishing Company, Inc.

Holocaust

Appleman-Jurman, A. (1990). Alicia: My story. New York: Bantam Books.

Bettelheim, B. (1960). The informed heart: Autonomy in a mass age. Glencoe, IL: Free Press.

DeSilva, C. (Ed.). (1993). In memory's kitchen: a legacy from the women of Terezín. Northvale, NJ: Jason Aronson

Fogelman, E. (1994). Conscience and courage: Rescuers of the Jews during the Holocaust. New York: Anchor Books.

Frankel, V. (1963). Man's search for meaning: An introduction to logotherapy. New York: Pocket Books. (Original work, From death camp to existentialism, published by Beacon Press, 1959.)

Friedman, N. (1998). A cup of honey: The story of a young Holocaust survivor, Eliezer Ayalon. Copyright 1999. Printed in Canada. All rights reserved.

Geier, A. (1998). Heroes of the Holocaust: Extraordinary true accounts of triumph. New York: Berkley Publishing Group.

Goldhagen, D. (1996). Hitler's willing executioners: Ordinary Germans and the Holocaust. New York: Alfred A. Knopf.

Gray, M. (1972). For those I loved. Boston: Little, Brown and Company.

Halter, M. (1998). Stories of deliverance: Speaking with men and women who rescued Jews from the Holocaust. Chicago: Open Court.

Helmreich, W. B. (1992). Against all odds: Holocaust survivors and the successful lives they made in America. New York: Simon & Schuster.

Jacobs, B. (2001). The dentist of Auschwitz: A memoir. Lexington, KY: The University Press of Kentucky.

Klemperer, V. (1999). I will bear witness: 1933-1941, a diary of the Nazi years. New York: The Modern Library.

Klemperer, V. (2001). I will bear witness: 1942-1945, a diary of the Nazi years. New York: The Modern Library.

Klein, G. W. (1995). All but my life. New York: Hill and Wang.

Lengyel, O. (1995). Five chimneys: The story of Auschwitz. Chicago: Academy Chicago Publishers.

Levi, P. (1987). The voice of memory: Interviews, 1961-1987. New York: The New Press.

Marks, J. (1995). The hidden children: The secret survivors of the Holocaust. New York: Ballantine Books.

Müller, F. (1979). Eyewitness Auschwitz. Chicago: Ivan R. De Publisher.

Nyiszli, M. (2011). Auschwitz: A doctor's eyewitness account. New York: Arcade Publishing.

Opdyke, I. (1999). In my hands: Memoirs of a Holocaust rescuer. New York: Knopf Books for Young Readers.

Roland, C. (1992). Courage under siege: Starvation, disease, and death in the Warsaw Ghetto. New York: Oxford University Press USA.

Schiff, H. (Ed.). (1995). Holocaust poetry. New York: St. Martin's Griffin.

Tec, N. (2003). Resilience and courage: Women, men, and the Holocaust. New Haven: The Yale University Press.

Ten Boom, C. (1971). The hiding place. New York: Bantam Books.

Wiesel, E. (1999). And the sea is never full. New York: Schocken Books.

Wilson, P. (Ed.) (1995). We are children just the same: Vedem, the secret magazine by the boys of Terezín. Philadelphia: The Jewish Publication Society.

Wisenthal, S. (1998). The sunflower: On the possibilities and limits of forgiveness. New York: Schocken Books.

Political Prisoners

Anderson, T. (1993). Den of lions: Memoirs of seven years. New York: Crown.

Bonhoeffer, D. (1971). Letters and papers from prison. New York: MacMillan Publishing Company

Gilkey, L. G. (1966). Shantung compound: The story of men and women under pressure. New York: Harper & Row.

Mandela, N. (1994). Long walk to freedom: The autobiography of Nelson Mandela. New York: Little, Brown & Company.

Sampson, A. (1999). Mandela: The authorized biography. New York: Alfred A. Knopf.

Solzhenitsyn, A. (1991). One day in the life of Ivan Denisovich. [5th translation by H. T. Willetts] New York: Noonday/Farrar Straus Giroux. (Original work published 1962).

Wu, H. (1995). Bitter winds: A memoir of my years in China's Gulag. New York: John Wiley & Sons.

War Stories

Levering, R. (1948). Horror trek: A true story of Bataan, the death march and three and one-half years in Japanese prison camps. Literary Licensing LLC. (Original publication date 1948.)

Nash, G. C. (1985). That we might live: A story of human triumph during World War II. Scottsdale, AZ: Shano Publishers. [Japanese internment camp, Philippines)

Rutledge, H. & Rutledge, P. (1973). In the presence of mine enemies: 1965-73 – A prisoner of war. Old Tappan, NJ: Fleming H. Revell Company. [Japanese POW, Philippines]

Stockdale, J. B. (1984). A Vietnam experience: Ten years of reflection. Stanford, CA: The Hoover Institution.

The History Channel (Producer). (1999). Secrets of World War II [documentary]. A&E Television Networks.

INDEX

A

African National Congress 53
Al 109, 164
Allen, Albert 35, 65, 83, 95, 104, 134, 163
Altmann, Judith 67, 73, 83, 84, 124, 132, 147, 149, 163
Anderson, Marian viii, ix
Ann 65, 78, 80, 100, 115, 116, 152, 153, 154, 163
apartheid 53, 55
Appel 26, 47, 80

B

Bataan 36, 58, 78, 95, 166, 172
Bill 37, 38, 39, 66, 67, 77, 102, 103, 121, 124, 164
Blumenfeld, Henry 163
Bob 57, 108, 124, 165

D

Diamond, Joe 9, 42, 57, 66, 68, 77, 85, 101, 108, 147, 149, 163

E

Ebner, Murray 69, 79, 99, 108, 126, 131, 160, 163
Ehrmann, Alex 20, 42, 46, 81, 148, 163

F

Feldman 167
Flying Tigers 71, 167
Formosa 60

G

generalized anxiety x, 7, 8
Geneva Convention 23, 28, 68, 96, 146
Germany viii, 8, 10, 16, 23, 26, 39, 40, 45, 84, 87, 89, 90, 91, 92, 93, 96,
    99, 103, 113, 122, 131, 144, 145, 146, 147, 153, 164, 165, 167
Gestalt 5, 6, 83, 157, 160, 166, 167
ghetto 1, 10, 20, 21, 25, 50, 51, 87, 109, 127, 142, 143, 152
Ginny 45, 46, 163

N

O

P

S

ACKNOWLEDGMENTS

To the survivors with whom I spoke, for their courage, their patience with the process, and their role in inspiring me to bring this project to fruition. The awe I feel for every survivor is mirrored by the awe I feel for their loved ones, waiting for them to come home. Months or years of anxiety were erased with each joyous reunion. However, for every happy ending, there were many others for whom there was either no homecoming at all or one where the anxiety of waiting was replaced by the anxiety of dealing with physical disabilities and/or post-traumatic stress issues in their loved one.

To Tommy Burkett, Lisbeth Lipari, Judith Thomas, and Katherine LaDu, who read early versions of the book.

To Karen Graves, Leslie Kern and George Williamson, for wading through what we thought at the time might be a final draft and courageously, even lovingly, telling us we were pretty far from final. Their wise observations gave us a clear direction to follow.

To Jack Shuler, for being a wise and caring mentor whose guidance led us to the end of the rainbow.

To Megan Owens, for standing in for three interviews that I was unable to cover.

To Liz Maher, our personal Sherlock Homes, for her invaluable research assistance and her ability to find anyone, anywhere!

To Debra Andreadis, Denison University Library, for helping us track down precise citations for references.

To Lyle Schmidt, my graduate advisor at The Ohio State University.

To Jep Carrell, for listening to me talk about creative problem-solving and coming up with the phrase, "spontaneous ingenuity."

To Ann Crowley-Hatten, for offering her technical expertise and advice on electronic ….

To Cheryl Meisterman, for being a supportive colleague through the years.

To Julia's children, spouses and grandchildren, whose encouragement through the years of this project ranged from gentle support to "Get that book published! Now!"

To Sandy's children, siblings and assorted friends for their wide-ranging support.

To our four-legged fans, who offered comfort and support through thick and thin: Julia's dogs, Lucky and Buddy, and Sandy's cats, Beau and Emmy.